PISCES

2004

PISCES
2004

Jane Struthers

p

This is a Parragon Book
First published in 2003

Parragon
Queen Street House
4 Queen Street
Bath BA1 1HE
UK

Produced by Magpie Books, an imprint of
Constable & Robinson Ltd, London

Illustrations courtesy of Slatter-Anderson, London
Cover courtesy of Simon Levy

ISBN 1-40541-567-3

A copy of the British Library Cataloguing-in-Publication Data
is available from the British Library

Printed and bound in the EU

CONTENTS

Introduction 1

Chapter One
The Year 2004 3

Chapter Two
Your Pisces Sun Sign 109

Chapter Three
Love and the Stars 115

Chapter Four
Your Astrological Holiday Guide 140

Chapter Five
Born on the Cusp? 148

Dates for 2004

Pisces 19 February – 20 March

Aries 21 March – 20 April

Taurus 21 April – 21 May

Gemini 22 May – 21 June

Cancer 22 June – 22 July

Leo 23 July – 23 August

Virgo 24 August – 23 September

Libra 24 September – 23 October

Scorpio 24 October – 22 November

Sagittarius 23 November – 21 December

Capricorn 22 December – 20 January

Aquarius 21 January – 18 February

INTRODUCTION

Dear Pisces

Happy New Year! I hope that 2004 is everything you want it to be, and more. If you're a clever Piscean you'll want to make the very best of the opportunities coming your way in the year ahead, which is why this book is so useful. It will help you to maximize your many chances and show you how to deal with any problem areas that you encounter.

My summary of 2004 in **The Year 2004** tells you exactly what you can expect in your relationships, health, money and career this year, and how to make the most of them. This is followed by my day-by-day forecasts for 2004, complete with at-a-glance charts that show you the general trend for each month.

Being born under the sign of Pisces gives you a special set of characteristics, and you can read all about them in **Your Pisces Sun Sign**. It's divided into four sections describing your relationships, health, money and career, so you can get a thorough insight into your personality. If some of your relationships have been puzzling you recently, you need to read **Love and the Stars** to discover what's going on. It describes your compatibility with each of the twelve signs, and is followed by two charts that show how you get on with the other signs in love and sex, and also as friends.

Everyone needs to get away from it all every now and then, and holidays can be good for our health. If you've ever wondered which is the ideal holiday for your Pisces Sun sign, turn to **Your Astrological Holiday Guide** to discover which destinations and activities will suit you best.

If you were born at the beginning or end of Pisces you may have always wondered if you're really a Piscean or whether you're an Aquarian or an Arien instead. Well, you can finally solve the mystery by turning to **Born on the Cusp?** and discovering which is your true Sun sign.

This book is all you need to get the very best out of 2004, so have fun and make it a great year!

Jane Struthers

THE YEAR 2004

Friends and Lovers

Congratulations! Your relationships blossom this year, leading to outbreaks of happiness and joy. The first nine months of 2004 are the best time to concentrate on all types of partnership, whether these involve love, sex, family connections, friendship or business. You'll flourish when you're with other people, and at times you may even feel happier with other people than when you're by yourself. This will be an excellent time to form a partnership with someone because it stands every chance of success.

Close and intimate relationships fare well from late September onwards. You'll enjoy one another's company and have lots of laughs into the bargain, which will come as a bonus. If you get involved with a lover now, they'll help to open up your life in all sorts of different ways and your world may never be the same again.

Throughout the year you'll feel very sensitive and at times your emotions will be quite fragile. You'll be highly attuned to the atmosphere around you, and especially aware of what's going on if a loved one doesn't have as much time for you as usual or they're being distant emotionally. Try not to make mountains out of molehills because there may be a very rational explanation for what's happening.

You've just embarked on a seven-year phase in which your world will change in many ways. All Pisceans will experience it at some point but you're most likely to be aware of it in 2004 if you were born between 18 and 26 February. You could be entranced by someone you meet now, or you may discover a different side to your personality and realize that it doesn't match your current lifestyle. So be prepared for anything to happen this year!

Health

Your energy levels will be erratic in 2004, fluctuating at times so that you feel up one day and down the next. This state of affairs will continue for some time to come, and it's important that you do your best to counter it by taking care of yourself and not burning the candle at both ends too often. It goes without saying that you should seek medical advice if you're worried about what's happening to you. You should also take a lot of care over your diet because that could have a big effect on your energy levels. You might become interested in unusual or unconventional diets, even if everyone around you tells you that you're bonkers. You'll also have a lot of nervous energy which you need to dispel, preferably by having regular and steady amounts of exercise and also by trying not to get too het up about anything.

You're no stranger to worry at the best of times but it's important not to allow anxieties to dominate your life in 2004. Given half the chance and a fertile imagination, any worries that are preying on you will become larger than life if you let them. It will be far better to take some constructive action over them and to face up to what's wrong than to pretend that nothing's happening.

Money

Given the radical changes that are starting to affect your life, your finances could go through rather bumpy phases in 2004. You may decide to throw in the towel with your current job before you look for another, so you have to fall back on your savings to get you through a lean period, or you might feel that you're coping with circumstances that are beyond your control. Do your best to be sensible by saving money rather than spending it whenever possible, and not doing anything rash until you've thought it through carefully.

If you're a typical Piscean you are very kind-hearted and this is a marvellous year for getting involved in some form of charity or voluntary work. You might decide to donate some of your money to a good cause, or to give up some of your spare time in order to work for a charity. You're also very susceptible to lame ducks and other people in need of help right now, but there may be times when you should avoid taking someone's story at face value in case they're trying to deceive you or rip you off. You should also avoid any shady or dodgy schemes like the plague or you'll come a cropper sooner or later.

If you want to turn over a new leaf in your financial matters or make a big investment, the best times to do so are the second half of April and the second half of October. Things will go very well for you, especially if you're making sensible and rational decisions.

Career

You'll fare best in your career if you take part in some sort of team work in 2004. You'll enjoy the company, for a start, and you'll also like bouncing your ideas off other people. You might even consider embarking on a business partnership with someone this year, in which case you should try to do so before the end of September in order to make the most of the prevailing astrological influences.

As a Piscean you are naturally creative and this is a marvellous year for demonstrating some of your talents. It's also a great time for learning new skills even if you aren't ready to show them to the waiting world just yet. Their time will come! If you've always wanted to paint, play the piano, write a novel or do anything else that appeals to you, give it your best shot now and see what happens.

Be careful when handling people in authority this year because they could be quite tricky. You don't want to get embroiled in battles for power if you can avoid them because they will be unpleasant and you'll arouse a lot of opposition in others. If you're in a position of power yourself, use it wisely and fairly, and don't let it go to your head.

Your Day by Day Guide

JANUARY AT A GLANCE

Love	♥ ♥ ♥
Money	£ $
Career	💻 💻 💻
Health	☼ ☼ ☼

• *Thursday 1 January* •

Happy New Year! Take things easy today because you aren't feeling nearly as upbeat and optimistic as you might like. In fact, you may even be feeling distinctly below par, and the stroppy attitude of a loved one won't help one bit. They seem determined to be difficult and obstructive, and they're also refusing to agree to some of your suggestions. All you can do is wait for this tricky phase to blow over.

• *Friday 2 January* •

Life is looking much more hopeful today, thank goodness, and you're more positive about what 2004 will bring. It's a super day for jotting down some of your New Year resolutions if you haven't yet done so, or for re-reading the ones you've already made. It's also a great day to get together with any friends or neighbours who you haven't seen recently.

• *Saturday 3 January* •

Chaos could break out at times this Saturday, thanks to domestic disruptions and changes of plan. You could have a surprise visitor who throws your routine out of whack, or who has some shocking news to impart. Be careful when handling fragile or precious objects to avoid breaking or damaging them, whether these are cherished ornaments or the egg you were just about to boil when you dropped it on the floor.

• *Sunday 4 January* •

Surround yourself with familiar faces and places today, or enjoy your home comforts with some special people. You don't feel in the slightest bit adventurous, so you won't want to deal with anything or anyone new. Ideally, you should settle down cosily with the Sunday papers, some delicious food and the reassuring presence of loved ones.

• *Monday 5 January* •

If you suspect that someone has been keeping things a secret from you, especially where money is concerned, you'll want to dig down to get to the truth now. This will be easier than you imagine, if you ask the right questions and don't come on too strong. You may find that it pays to feign indifference, even though you're really hanging on to someone's every word.

• *Tuesday 6 January* •

Let your hair down and live a little! You're in an excitable and sociable mood, making you yearn to have fun. If the day's plans are tedious enough to make you dislocate your jaw with bored yawns, think about how you can liven things up. But don't be surprised if fate takes a hand and you're offered the chance to do something on the spur of the moment. It will be great!

• *Wednesday 7 January* •

Today's Full Moon is reminding you that it's about time you did something constructive about you-know-who. Maybe you're worried about a child's welfare and are wondering what to do about it, or there's been a rift with a loved one and you're longing to kiss and make up with them. Whatever is wrong, you should tackle it during the coming fortnight.

• *Thursday 8 January* •

Try not to organize any social events today because there's a strong possibility that they'll go haywire. For instance, a date to get together with friends may have to be postponed, or there might be no sign of the table you booked when you turn up at the restaurant. You also won't get very far now if you try to have a serious conversation with a loved one.

• *Friday 9 January* •

This is a fantastic day for making plans that you can look forward to, especially if they involve some sort of social activity. Maybe you could arrange a big gathering with some of your chums, or you'll decide to visit someone who lives a long way away. If you've been waiting for the right moment to break the ice with someone you'd like to know better, you will have the perfect opportunity to do so.

• *Saturday 10 January* •

Your feelings are very near the surface today, making you sensitive to what's going on around you. Take care because you could easily start to feel rather hard-done-by if things don't go your way or you suspect that you've been put in an inferior position. The trouble is that things could soon assume massive proportions and spoil your day, making you feel like Cinderella when she's told she can't go to the ball.

• *Sunday 11 January* •

You're in a much more resilient and steady mood today, enabling you to cope with whatever comes along. Luckily, this looks like being an easy and satisfying day, especially if you can talk to loved ones about whatever is on your mind at the moment. You'll manage to create a strong rapport with them, and you'll feel that they're utterly dependable.

• *Monday 12 January* •

It would be a shame to spend too much time alone today because you're in such an outgoing frame of mind. You'll enjoy mixing with people whenever you get the chance, whether they're your greatest buddies or a stranger standing next to you in the supermarket queue. If you're taking part in a group activity you'll enjoy yourself and may even be asked to take the helm at some point.

• *Tuesday 13 January* •

Someone is in a nit-picking and pedantic mood today, making them a real pain in the neck. Not that you would dare to say so, of course, because you'd only get an earful, and such comments may not even be appropriate if this person is in a position of authority over you. However, you'll show your displeasure in some way or other, perhaps by being sarcastic or monosyllabic.

• *Wednesday 14 January* •

Good news! You'll be exerting a magnetic attraction for lots of people over the next three weeks, with your popularity rising by several degrees. Just what you need to brighten up what is often a rather miserable time of year! It's also the perfect excuse to splash out on some new clothes, a more flattering hairstyle, or anything else that will enhance your appearance.

• *Thursday 15 January* •

Love has some surprises in store for you today. You might be powerfully attracted to someone who wouldn't normally do a thing for you, or an existing partner might dazzle you with their magnetism. You'll also enjoy displaying a different side of your personality from usual and the more unexpected this is, the bigger impact it will have on everyone who witnesses it.

• *Friday 16 January* •

Get together with people who are on the same wavelength as you today, especially if you're all working towards a joint aim. For instance, you'll enjoy talking to people who share your ideas about politics, religion or ecology, or anything else that you consider to be an essential part of life. You might also hear from someone who lives abroad.

• *Saturday 17 January* •

This is a wonderfully gregarious day, and it's perfect for being with friends and other kindred spirits. You might even make a new chum now if you're feeling brave enough to get talking to someone who looks as though they could be fun. At some point today it's a good idea to concentrate on your hopes and wishes for the future and to renew your belief in them.

• *Sunday 18 January* •

Someone could easily get carried away with the sound of their own voice today, making them bang on endlessly about how wonderful they are. You won't really mind, and you may even be secretly amused by their astonishing amount of self-confidence, but you should certainly avoid getting drawn into some sort of competition over who is most successful or popular.

• *Monday 19 January* •

This is a great day for doing things on the spur of the moment. You don't want to feel that you're ruled by your routine or restricted by the expectations of others, and you'll be happiest if you're allowed to do your own thing now. You're also feeling slightly independent and may opt for some time on your own rather than being glued to someone else's side.

• *Tuesday 20 January* •

This is a fantastic day for getting things done and telling people what you think, because you're forceful, dynamic and powerful right now. However, it's essential that you avoid letting this go to your head, making you insist on having things all your own way. You must work in tandem with others in order to get the best results now, and not be the one who calls all the shots.

• *Wednesday 21 January* •

If you play your cards right you'll be able to establish a strong rapport with a certain person today, and feel that you can draw on it in the months to come. If a relationship has been a little dicey lately, this is your chance to mend it by finding out what's been going on and then doing what you can to remedy the situation. The results will be even better than you dared hope.

• *Thursday 22 January* •

A loved one is being awfully critical and harsh today, making you wonder if you can put a foot right. Unfortunately, this will become a vicious circle if you aren't careful, with you feeling beleaguered by this person's miserable mood and them making the most of it. Even if they have a valid point, their current behaviour is simply putting you on the defensive.

• *Friday 23 January* •

You're acting on whims today, making you seem very erratic and possibly even eccentric. You will also struggle to keep your mind on anything for very long because you'll soon be distracted by something else. You're being driven by sudden urges that make you do things on the spur of the moment, but you must avoid rushing into hasty decisions that you haven't thought through properly.

• *Saturday 24 January* •

Charm is spilling out of you today, making people flock to your side like bees around a flower. You could hear lots of wonderful compliments, or someone might buy you a present that has you blushing with pleasure. Romance won't be far away, either, whether you're swept off your feet by someone or you're indulging in some delicious escapism by watching a favourite film.

• *Sunday 25 January* •

You have high hopes of someone today but will they be realized? Unfortunately, you'll be disappointed if you're being unrealistic about what this person can do for you or how they feel about you. Your high expectations may also blind you to the fact that things are actually going very well with this person, even though they don't seem this way at the moment.

• *Monday 26 January* •

No matter what else you're doing today, you'll enjoy devoting a little time to some of your priorities in life. Maybe you'll get together with someone who always makes you happy, or perhaps you'll do something that makes you feel good. For instance, if you love nature you might buy yourself a bunch of the most beautiful flowers you can lay your hands on.

• *Tuesday 27 January* •

This is an excellent day for talking about anything that is currently bothering you, provided that you choose a suitable confidant, of course. It's also a brilliant chance to get to grips with your finances, perhaps by paying a few bills or balancing your chequebook. Taking care of such tasks will make you feel that you're in control of your life, even if you aren't really!

• *Wednesday 28 January* •

Money could cause problems today, provoking someone into losing their temper or going into a moody sulk. Maybe you're annoyed at the way a certain person seems to be squandering their cash on rubbish, or perhaps the boot's on the other foot and they're angry about your spending habits. A row seems likely, so use it to clear the air rather than to prolong the argument.

• *Thursday 29 January* •

Pleasure and love are your main priorities today, and everything else will have to take a back seat. Not very good news if you're supposed to be slogging your guts out at work, because you'll find any excuse not to do this. Instead, you'll want to be with people who make your heart beat that little bit faster, or whose presence is an essential part of your life.

• *Friday 30 January* •

If you've got some spare time you'll enjoy walking around your local surroundings today, chatting to whoever you meet. Grab the chance to butter up a tricky neighbour, make a date to see a friend or keep up with the latest gossip. You'll also have fun if you're doing some window-shopping, although this could quickly turn into real shopping if you see something you like.

• *Saturday 31 January* •

You've got a lot to say for yourself and so have your friends. This means it's a super day for getting involved in discussions and far-reaching conversations, and for keeping the atmosphere light and polite throughout. If you've been wondering about joining a society or organization that caters for one of your interests, you may decide to take the plunge now and you'll be very glad that you did.

FEBRUARY AT A GLANCE

Love	♥ ♥ ♥ ♥ ♥
Money	£ $ £ $
Career	💻 💻 💻 💻 💻
Health	☼ ☼ ☼ ☼ ☼

• *Sunday 1 February* •

Tensions are never far from the surface today, making it hard to maintain your equilibrium for long. You may feel that someone is getting at you or that they're doing all they can to resist what you're trying to achieve. Try not to tell yourself that this is an all-or-nothing situation – that will just send you into a panic. You need to find a compromise soon, but there's nothing doing right now.

• *Monday 2 February* •

If you're a typical Piscean, you have a strong need to disappear into your own little world every now and then, and this Monday is a shining example of that. Ideally, you should be left to your own devices for as long as you want, allowing you to mull things over, listen to music or simply stare at the carpet. You're also busily avoiding reality but you'll have to make yourself face up to this sooner or later.

• *Tuesday 3 February* •

Between now and late March you'll enjoy keeping on the move as much as possible, whether this simply means being more active on a day-to-day basis or taking off on short trips. If you can't do things like this you'll soon get bored, restless and distinctly edgy, which could lead to some heated arguments and tetchy moments. And you don't want that, do you?

• *Wednesday 4 February* •

You're at your most affectionate and demonstrative today, which is really saying something, so don't let these warm feelings go to waste. It's a glorious opportunity to be with some of your favourite people, or perhaps all you need is one person in particular. You're also very creative now and will love expressing yourself artistically.

• *Thursday 5 February* •

Someone is impatient and hasty today, making it difficult to be around them for long without catching the sharp edge of their tongue. They seem to be in a tearing hurry, which they think gives them the excuse to be rude or abrupt with you, or even to push you out of the way when necessary. If you tick them off the situation is likely to escalate into a row, but what else can you do?

• *Friday 6 February* •

You're in a go-getting mood and you won't like it if you can't do what you want, when you want. You're also eager to get as many things done in as short a time as possible, and you could even be tempted to cut corners if you think no one will notice. But is this really such a good idea, Pisces? Watch out for bouts of carelessness, especially if you're driving.

• *Saturday 7 February* •

Over the next couple of weeks there will be phases when you're reluctant to say what you think, or even to say much at all. You'll much prefer to keep your head down and keep your thoughts to yourself, but there may be times when this strategy is self-defeating or makes others suspicious of what you might be up to. So sometimes you'll have to force yourself to speak up.

• *Sunday 8 February* •

You're moving into a rather extravagant period in which you'll want to splash your money around in all directions, whether or not you can afford to do so. Once you clap eyes on something that you want to buy, it will be almost impossible to resist it. Nevertheless, this will be a super time for buying items that will bring pleasure, relaxation or beauty into your life.

• *Monday 9 February* •

Watch out right now because you have a nasty habit of blurting out things that would have been better left unsaid. For instance, you may be desperately trying not to mention someone's name or raise a particular topic, and then find that you've done the very thing you were trying so hard to avoid. The more agitated or annoyed you feel, the more likely this is to happen. So calm down!

• *Tuesday 10 February* •

You're feeling unappreciated and alone, and it's making you miserable. What's wrong? It's highly likely that there's been a breach between you and a loved one, or that you're physically separated from one another at the moment, and it's getting you down. You're feeling sorry for yourself so it's tempting to imagine that things are worse than they really are, but it won't do you any good to mope like this.

• *Wednesday 11 February* •

This is a terrific day to fix problems and improve difficult situations. You'll enjoy the opportunity to do some trouble-shooting, especially if you're sorting out things that have been weighing on your mind for some time now. It's also an excellent day to confide in someone whose wisdom and experience you respect, and who can give you the back-up you need.

• *Thursday 12 February* •

Keep a watchful eye open for anyone who thinks they've got right on their side, or that they're being politically correct, because they'll find any excuse to tick you off, correct you or clamber on to their soapbox. You'll soon get fed up with this sort of holier-than-thou behaviour, but beware of sounding equally pious if you start to tell them what you think of them.

• *Friday 13 February* •

Today is a continuation of yesterday's tense atmosphere, with the distinct impression that you need to police everything you say in case someone finds fault with it. You may also have another bout of foot-in-mouth disease, in which you say the very thing you were hoping to keep quiet about. Be careful not to divulge something that was supposed to remain a secret.

• *Saturday 14 February* •

Well, it may be Valentine's Day but you'll have to work hard to create a romantic atmosphere. That's because there's a strong air of constraint and distance between you and your beloved now, or so it seems to you. You can get over this if you try, and if you can resist the temptation to take problems to heart and brood about them, but this could be quite a tall order right now.

• *Sunday 15 February* •

Life is very confusing today. You're being bombarded with thoughts and impressions, making it hard to work out what's really happening and what's simply your imagination. It doesn't help that you're showing a tendency to believe only what you want to believe and to disregard anything unpleasant or challenging. How long can you sweep all this under the mental carpet?

• *Monday 16 February* •

It's another day when you're feeling extremely sensitive. You might also be wary of someone, which is putting you on your guard and making you uncomfortable. Perhaps you've got to spend time with someone you aren't sure of, and you're waiting for them to be critical or unpleasant towards you, or you're anxious about letting yourself down in some way. Come on, Pisces, relax!

• *Tuesday 17 February* •

Your positive emotions are in marked contrast to yesterday's miserable mood and you're feeling much more outgoing and friendly. This will come as a great relief, and it will also encourage lots of people to get in touch with you. If you haven't yet got anything planned for the weekend, consider arranging something enjoyable now, so you can look forward to it.

• *Wednesday 18 February* •

Someone is in a rather grumpy and crotchety mood, making it difficult to spend much time with them without getting your head bitten off. Maybe they're stewing about something and are looking for any outlet for their aggression, or perhaps they're annoyed with you in particular. It will be far better to get things out into the open than to allow this situation to drag on.

• *Thursday 19 February* •

Your energy levels start to rise from today and they'll have a very positive effect on your mood over the coming four weeks. This will be a super opportunity to take the initiative in any way that seems necessary, whether this is getting a new relationship off the ground, starting an exciting venture or adopting a healthier regime.

• *Friday 20 February* •

You're in the mood to spend money today, which could work out expensive because you won't be interested in counting the cost. In fact, you'll want to ignore such unpleasant facts as whether or not you can afford something. Even so, if you can spare the money you'll enjoy buying items that appeal to your senses, such as some perfume, soap or sensual fabrics.

• *Saturday 21 February* •

You have high hopes of someone this Saturday but you could be disappointed if you've overestimated what they're capable of. Maybe you're hoping that they'll make some grand emotional gesture towards you, even though you know full well that this isn't their style or they aren't in a position to do so. You'll be happier if you can be realistic about what can and can't happen.

• *Sunday 22 February* •

You long to assert your independence and prove that you're different from the rest of the crowd today, especially if life is getting rather boring or predictable. You could be inspired to buy some clothes that make a very definite statement or which are designed to raise eyebrows. What's more, you're feeling restless and it will be hard to settle down to anything for long.

• *Monday 23 February* •

Concentrate on people and activities that give you pleasure today. For instance, you might want to make a date to see someone special, even if you can only manage a few minutes with them, or you could visit a favourite art gallery in your lunch hour. Such activities will remind you that life is worth living, even if things are rather tough at the moment.

• *Tuesday 24 February* •

A certain person is an awkward customer today, so treat them carefully. Be very wary about believing everything they tell you because there's a strong possibility that they're keeping some vital information to themselves or they're trying to hide the fact that they haven't done something they were supposed to. Proceed with caution!

• *Wednesday 25 February* •

This is a marvellous day for doing some forward planning, especially if you're trying to organize a social event or big celebration. You'll make a lot of satisfying progress now, and other people will be surprisingly helpful and co-operative. If you've got to stick within a strict budget you'll still manage to get value for money and to put on a good show.

• *Thursday 26 February* •

Today's a super day for putting across your point of view in a way that makes everyone sit up and take notice, because your words will pack quite a punch this Thursday. You'll even manage to hold your own when talking to people who don't agree with you, instead of collapsing in an apologetic heap and letting others steamroller you into submission. And it feels great!

• *Friday 27 February* •

So many thoughts and ideas are rushing through your mind that it's almost impossible to keep track of them today. You might also wonder whether they're worth noting down because they're so wacky, controversial or ahead of their time. Well, you won't know until you try, so jot down your ideas in case they come in handy later on. Some could even be strokes of genius.

• *Saturday 28 February* •

Domestic matters are fraught today, with loved ones being awkward or spoiling for a row. Or perhaps you're the one with a bee in your bonnet, especially if you're fretting about something that happened in the past? Take care, because it's one of those days in which it's easy to let resentments eat away at you and put you in a highly subjective, and unreasonable, mood.

• *Sunday 29 February* •

It's a great day to turn your thoughts in practical directions because you've definitely got your head screwed on the right way. You're happy to deal with the facts without losing sight of other important considerations, such as happiness and comfort. You'll also excel at creative or artistic pastimes.

MARCH AT A GLANCE

Love	♥ ♥ ♥ ♥ ♥
Money	£ $ £ $ £
Career	💻 💻 💻 💻
Health	☼ ☼ ☼ ☼ ☼

• *Monday 1 March* •

It's a super start to March because you're in a very happy and cheerful mood. You're determined to enjoy yourself, and even if you usually spend Mondays at home the prospect of a social outing is far too tempting to resist. Right now, you feel like going out on the town or inviting someone round to your place, and nothing less will do.

• *Tuesday 2 March* •

It's another good day when you feel gregarious and affable. You'll love being with people who are on the same wavelength as you, or perhaps making a special effort to do something nice with your other half. This is particularly important if you normally take each other slightly for granted or your relationship has a tendency to get rather stale.

• *Wednesday 3 March* •

You're in the mood for some soothing retail therapy, especially if this isn't a very easy day or you're having problems with a certain person. You'll feel so much better if you can have a quick tour of your favourite shops, even if you're really supposed to be saving money rather than spending it. But try not to end up out of pocket because that will only make you feel worse in the long run.

• *Thursday 4 March* •

Someone may not intend to do it but they could get very carried away today and make promises that they can't keep. They're likely to be saying things that they think you want to hear or which show them in a good light, so you'll have to read between the lines and try to find the truth in what you're hearing.

• *Friday 5 March* •

You're on great form socially over the next few weeks, so make the most of this convivial patch while it lasts. Mind you, this may happen of its own accord, perhaps because you receive lots of tempting invitations or get involved in a local activity that introduces you to many new faces. Love might also blossom with a neighbour now.

• *Saturday 6 March* •

Today's Full Moon will have a powerful impact on your relationships over the next two weeks, urging you to take constructive action and deal with any connections that are causing you problems at the moment. You may have to be tough with someone or lay down some ground rules, so they understand that you aren't going to be messed around any longer.

• *Sunday 7 March* •

You feel that you've got to tread carefully with a certain person today in order to stop them going into a massive sulk. Yet this is emotional blackmail, and if you play ball you'll be allowing them to manipulate and control you. Do you really want this to happen, or are you prepared to be straight with this person and risk incurring their displeasure? It won't be an easy choice.

• *Monday 8 March* •

If you've been thinking over what happened yesterday, it's highly likely that you've now decided that you aren't going to stand for this bad behaviour any longer and you're going to put your foot down. Well, this is definitely the day to do it because you're capable of making some tough statements when necessary, even if your knees are trembling or your voice goes all wobbly. Good for you!

• *Tuesday 9 March* •

Life keeps you on your toes today, with plenty of unexpected events to deal with. They won't be anything to worry about and could even be great fun, so don't panic. You might receive an invitation out of the blue, or bump into the last person you were expecting to see. There could also be a light-hearted flirtation with a certain someone who sets you wondering about what's going on between you.

• *Wednesday 10 March* •

Pay plenty of attention to the women in your life today. Otherwise they could start to feel neglected and become rather demanding. If you're organizing a social event and there's a question mark over whether to invite a certain person or not, you'll have to think things through carefully to avoid giving offence.

• *Thursday 11 March* •

You're in an enterprising and adventurous mood, so you won't want to do anything that's too tedious or pedestrian. Instead, you're eager to branch out in new directions, especially if this will involve travel or education. Many things seem possible at the moment, thereby increasing your options and giving you fresh hope for the future. It's all very encouraging!

• *Friday 12 March* •

Have a serious think about your long-term goals today, especially if you're wondering how to turn some of them into reality. You'll have to ask yourself some tough questions, such as whether you're barking up the wrong tree with some of these objectives. Even if you're sure of what to do, you could be facing considerable opposition from other quarters.

• *Saturday 13 March* •

The questions that you were grappling with yesterday continue to bother you today, but with less intensity. Perhaps you've managed to solve some of your problems or someone is now less determined to stand in your way. Nevertheless, this won't be an easy day because you'll feel fraught and geared up for a row at the first hint of conflict.

• *Sunday 14 March* •

You're in for a tricky time today, caused by disagreements over someone's spare-time activities or the company they keep. For instance, they may spend so much time on a hobby that you barely see them, or perhaps they're being far too spendthrift for your liking. What you must remember in all this is that you're seeing things from a very subjective and emotional viewpoint.

• *Monday 15 March* •

Keep clear of someone who wants to prove a point because they'll do so by being highly critical of you. They might pick holes in everything you do or say, or make sarcastic comments that are designed to make you feel uncomfortable. To make matters worse, you may be worrying about a financial matter or a relationship, so you're very vulnerable to criticism and inclined to take it all too much to heart.

• *Tuesday 16 March* •

This is a marvellous day for putting plans into action, whether they're modest or major. You're all geared up to make things happen and you're excited about what you might be able to achieve right now. Get out your list of New Year resolutions if you haven't looked at it lately, and decide where you're going to start with them all.

• *Wednesday 17 March* •

Fun and pleasure are your watchwords today, and you won't be very pleased if these are in short supply. You're eager to enjoy yourself whenever you get the chance, particularly if you can go out on the town or meet up with some kindred spirits. If you're going out on a date with you-know-who, things should go exactly the way you want.

• *Thursday 18 March* •

You'll enjoy keeping busy today. This will help you to burn up lots of nervous energy that might otherwise make you rather fractious or restless. Visit the gym, go for a jog or have a blitz on the garden. You're feeling decisive at the moment and you won't like it if you're supposed to back-pedal on something because you'd much rather go in with all guns blazing.

• *Friday 19 March* •

You're wearing rose-tinted spectacles today, making it difficult for you to see situations in their true light. You could be putting a very favourable spin on something that isn't nearly as good as you think, or burying your head in the sand about a problem that you wish would go away of its own accord. This isn't a good day for making important decisions because you aren't being realistic.

• *Saturday 20 March* •

Focus on whatever or whoever makes your world go round over the next few weeks. Promise yourself that you'll devote a little time each day to something that makes you happy, even if you have to get up earlier in order to fit it in. This will also be an excellent period for investing money in items that will grow in value or bring you a lot of pleasure over the years.

• *Sunday 21 March* •

Between now and early May you should channel plenty of energy into your domestic and family life. This could be your cue to start the long process of moving house or doing up your current home, or to create a magical haven out of the mess that's supposed to be your garden. It has to be said that there will also be times when loved ones tend to get under your skin and provoke you.

• *Monday 22 March* •

Have a think about whether you should be buying items that will make you more efficient or impressive. For instance, you might decide to upgrade your current computer program so you can take advantage of the latest improvements, or you may realize that you need to buy some smart clothes for work.

• *Tuesday 23 March* •

The more flexible you can be today, the more you'll enjoy yourself and be able to take the day's events in your stride. This will be very handy if you have to adapt to changing situations or need to stay on the right side of someone who likes to keep you on your toes. It's also a good day for chatting to friends or getting involved in an intellectual discussion.

• *Wednesday 24 March* •

You're able to put forward your ideas with complete conviction and assurance today, which is just what you need if you're hoping to talk someone into seeing things from your point of view. You'll be able to state your case with authority, without getting into a flap or turning the entire encounter into an excuse for an emotional outburst.

• *Thursday 25 March* •

Get out the kid gloves because you're going to need them today when dealing with a certain someone. It seems that they're looking for an argument and will do whatever they can to make it happen. They may goad you into losing your temper or resurrect all sorts of past resentments as though they've only just happened. By the looks of it, a row is almost inevitable.

• *Friday 26 March* •

You're feeling rather down in the mouth, with a tendency to take a pessimistic view of anything that's bothering you at the moment, even if this isn't justified. All you can do is try to remain realistic and not to panic. Something else that will help is keeping away from people who take a perverse delight in making you feel even more wretched or worried than you do already.

• *Saturday 27 March* •

Take care because your feelings are easily churned up today, leading to some very uncomfortable moments. For instance, you might feel such profound anger that you don't know what to do about it, or you could have a sense of dread about something that has yet to happen. You may also have to cope with a loved one who is trying to manipulate your emotions. What a day!

• *Sunday 28 March* •

Family life is fraught with problems, which will be a nuisance if you were looking forward to a cosy day with your nearest and dearest. Someone may have a point to prove, in which case they'll do it in the most disruptive or attention-seeking way they can find. Or all your careful plans might fall apart when someone moves the goalposts or drops a last-minute bombshell. Yikes!

• *Monday 29 March* •

Life has been rather fraught over the past few days but you can breathe a big sigh of relief now because you're entering a much more favourable and easy-going phase. Celebrate by making contact with friends or by going out with your partner. If you're smitten by someone and are hoping that they feel the same way about you, you'll have fresh cause for hope now.

• *Tuesday 30 March* •

This is a glorious day for being as sociable as possible. Not only will you enjoy yourself, but everyone you meet will feel all the better for seeing you. You might hear some ego-boosting compliments or receive an invitation that you'll really look forward to. If you're going shopping you'll enjoy buying items that will enhance your appearance in some way.

• *Wednesday 31 March* •

Your work situation looks good this Wednesday. Colleagues and customers are being friendly and helpful, and you'll return the compliment. You might even receive a nice little bonus or tip from someone who's pleased with your work, or you'll hear encouraging news about a pay rise that's on the way. You'll also take great satisfaction in doing jobs to the best of your ability now.

APRIL AT A GLANCE

Love	♥ ♥ ♥
Money	£ $ £ $ £
Career	🖳 🖳
Health	☼ ☼

• Thursday 1 April •

You'll be at your most voluble and articulate over the next few days, so don't be surprised if you're much more chatty than usual. You'll have an opinion on almost every subject, whether you know anything about it or not, and will really enjoy holding forth on it. Local activities will appeal now, not least because they'll give you the chance to find out what's going on in your immediate surroundings. You could hear some great gossip!

• Friday 2 April •

Someone is being really difficult today, so be prepared for some tricky moments with them. They're in a bad mood and don't care who they take it out on, provided that they can let off a little steam whenever they feel it's necessary. There could also be a dispute about a family or domestic matter, with everyone getting unnecessarily hot under the collar. Do your best to stay calm and not blow a gasket at the first sign of a problem.

• *Saturday 3 April* •

If things became rather dicey with loved ones yesterday, you'll be able to put matters to rights over the next couple of weeks. Don't be too proud to make amends if you think you've stepped out of line or done something upsetting. On a lighter note, this will be a super opportunity to put your tremendous artistic skills to good use in your home or garden, especially if you want to create a haven of peace for yourself.

• *Sunday 4 April* •

You're very tuned in to your values and priorities in life this Sunday, and will happily devote as much time to them as possible. This means that you won't be interested in anything that feels like a chore or which requires too much hard work on your part. Take care if you're handling money: it could easily slip through your fingers without you being aware of it.

• *Monday 5 April* •

Today's Full Moon will trigger a few financial hiccups over the coming fortnight, so watch out! If you've been spending money like water, you'll soon notice that a drought has set in and that you've got to do something about it. This will also be an excellent period in which to sort out important or official papers, to pay outstanding bills and generally to get things shipshape.

• *Tuesday 6 April* •

Enthusiasm carries you along on the crest of an exciting wave today, but don't go overboard or it will dash you on to the rocks. For instance, you might decide to do something energetic and then not know when to stop, so you end up with aching bones and muscles. A little moderation won't go amiss, even though it's the last thing on your mind right now.

• *Wednesday 7 April* •

You're in a terrific mood and long may it last. You're feeling upbeat, gregarious and keen on having a good laugh. It's a super day for being sociable and mixing with like-minded people. There could also be an interesting or encouraging conversation with someone who comes from another country or culture.

• *Thursday 8 April* •

You hate the prospect of being restricted in any way today, and you'll do your best to escape from what you see as unnecessary limitations. This might mean putting off your work until you're more in the mood for it, ducking out of an obligation, or simply wanting to rebel against people who are trying to tell you what to do. Right now, you need as much freedom as you can get.

• *Friday 9 April* •

Loved ones are hard to handle and potentially hurtful this Friday. Someone wants to do their own thing without being hampered by anyone else, which will make you feel vulnerable, rejected and left out in the cold. If you're the one who needs room to breathe, try not to behave in ways that cause unnecessary distress and hurt to others.

• *Saturday 10 April* •

You're taking things very much to heart right now, so bear that in mind if you start to get agitated or upset. Problems that seem monumental, or even insurmountable, to you at the moment will soon return to more reasonable proportions. In the meantime, however, you'll have to wrestle with emotional upsets, possible paranoia and a jarring sense of being out of control.

• *Sunday 11 April* •

This is a good day for taking yourself in hand and giving yourself a good talking-to, especially if yesterday was hard work. The best way to find out what's going on in your life is to examine it in as much detail as possible, and maybe also to confide in someone you trust. You're in a good position to regain power and control over what's happening to you.

• *Monday 12 April* •

Money and friends don't mix today, so try to keep them as far apart as possible. If you lend money or a possession to someone, there could be a problem about getting it back, leading to resentment and irritation. There might also be a dispute about a forthcoming social event or a group gathering, with everyone looking for reasons to get uppity and scratchy.

• *Tuesday 13 April* •

This is a marvellous day for getting to the bottom of secrets and finding out exactly what's going on around you. You might be able to coax a loved one into confiding in you or baring their soul, provided that you're able to treat what they tell you with discretion and respect. It's also a great day for having a good tidy-up at home and rediscovering items that you thought you'd lost for ever.

• Wednesday 14 April •

Gather some of your loved ones around you because it's a wonderful day for enjoying yourself. Actually, that's the only thing you're in the mood for, and you'll try to put as much distance between yourself and hard work as possible. You'll be the life and soul of any party you attend, and might even be inspired to organize something on the spur of the moment.

• Thursday 15 April •

Loved ones need a lot of attention and love today. If they don't get it, they'll make it plain that they're feeling neglected and may cause mini scenes until they receive whatever it is they're looking for. If you're busy around your home you'll enjoy showing off your domestic skills, perhaps by baking a cake, cooking a delicious meal or creating a safe and cosy atmosphere.

• Friday 16 April •

A loved one needs careful handling because they're poised on the brink of losing their temper. This will make you feel that you've got to tiptoe around them to avoid upsetting them, even though that's probably a waste of time because they'll find an excuse to get angry no matter what you do. Ask them to tell you what's wrong, in case you can help in some way.

• Saturday 17 April •

This is a super day for talking about whatever happens to be important to you at the moment. This might be a person, a belief, a possession or an activity, but whatever it is you need to discuss it with other people. If no one is interested in hearing what you've got to say, perhaps you could put your thoughts down on paper instead.

• *Sunday 18 April* •

You'll get an enormous amount of pleasure from pottering about at home and enjoying your creature comforts this Sunday. You won't want to stray too far from familiar surroundings, and nor will you be very enthusiastic about meeting people for the first time. A walk in the park, a stroll in a favourite stretch of countryside or a snooze in your garden will help to relax you.

• *Monday 19 April* •

Today's eclipsed New Moon will have a dramatic impact on your finances between now and early May. This could be really good news, heralding the arrival of a windfall or something else that swells the coffers. It's certainly a marvellous opportunity to make sensible investments, and also to make the best possible use of your time.

• *Tuesday 20 April* •

Life keeps you busy today and you may even struggle to fit everything into your timetable. Stand by for some unexpected developments, such as a surprise visitor or a last-minute change of plan. It will be good fun not knowing what's around the corner, so do your best to be as flexible, open-minded and spontaneous as possible.

• *Wednesday 21 April* •

You have a very high opinion of loved ones at the moment and want to see them in the best possible light. You may even turn a blind eye to some glaring faults, perhaps because you're reluctant to admit to yourself that a certain person is only human. Beware of idolizing anyone: you'll be bitterly disappointed later on when you realize that they have feet of clay.

• *Thursday 22 April* •

You're in a great mood and you're keen to spread a little happiness wherever you go. You're just the tonic for anyone who's feeling down in the mouth because you'll soon cheer them up and give them something to smile about. What's more, you're taking a very positive approach to your own situation and will find the silver lining to any cloud that's currently hovering over you.

• *Friday 23 April* •

A certain someone seems to have got out of bed on the wrong side, and now they're taking it out on anyone who happens to be within firing range. They're being moody and emotionally demanding, much to your annoyance. Do your best not to become infected by their irritable emotions, or you'll soon be bickering and quarrelling with each other.

• *Saturday 24 April* •

Be very careful when dealing with people in power and authority today because they're throwing their weight around and they won't like it if you stand up to them. Yet you won't like the way they're calling the shots and bossing you about. Matching might with might isn't the answer, and could even make the situation more fraught and difficult than it is already.

• *Sunday 25 April* •

You need to introduce as much flexibility and variety into your day as possible to avoid getting bored, fed up or mentally stultified. It will also help if you can be with people who are lively and have some interesting things to say. Try to keep away from anyone who feels duty bound to toe the line or be ultra-conventional because they'll really get on your nerves.

• *Monday 26 April* •

Loved ones are taking things very personally, so watch what you say if you want to avoid upsetting them. Try to keep things light and easy-going, and to bear in mind that everyone is being rather subjective at the moment. This isn't a good day for reaching decisions because you're showing a tendency to chop and change your mind whenever the fancy takes you.

• *Tuesday 27 April* •

It's a tricky day and patience is thin on the ground. The better you know someone, the greater their tendency to annoy you right now, which will lead to some tense scenes when dealing with close relatives, neighbours and colleagues. Do your best to rise above an impulse that makes you want to snap at people, or to be curt or sarcastic when talking to them.

• *Wednesday 28 April* •

This is a super day for getting things done because you're highly efficient and organized. If you want to make every second count, plan your time in advance. It will be surprisingly easy to concentrate on whatever you're doing, and also to put your thoughts into words. Right now you want to be treated with respect, and that's exactly what will happen.

• *Thursday 29 April* •

Relationships are slightly fraught today, so proceed with caution. A partner wants to do things in their own way and in their own time, without any reference to you. You may also have to deal with someone who keeps blowing hot and cold, so you don't know whether you're in favour or out of it. The best way to handle this behaviour is to let it wash over you and not to take it personally.

• *Friday 30 April* •

You're feeling highly sociable and gregarious this Friday, so it would be a shame if you had to spend too much time on your own. Ideally, you should get together with friends and relatives, or make a big effort to do something nice with your other half. Any form of negotiation or discussion will go well now, so it's a super day to put across your point of view.

MAY AT A GLANCE

Love	♥ ♥ ♥
Money	£ $
Career	💻
Health	☼ ☼

• *Saturday 1 May* •

You can make a lot of progress with a certain person today if you play your cards right. This means being constructive and helpful while also keeping your feet on the ground. Be prepared to talk about your differences because this will be the best way for you to meet in the middle and not to allow any problems to assume massive proportions.

• *Sunday 2 May* •

Someone has a tremendous drive for personal or emotional power today, making them quite a force to be reckoned with.

They could easily use manipulative or even underhand tactics in order to get what they want, leaving you feeling like a pawn in their game of chess. You'll want to stand up to them but be careful how you do this. Above all, resist the temptation to give as good as you get – that will only make matters worse.

• *Monday 3 May* •

Financial matters are rather fraught today, so tread carefully. You'll be strongly influenced by everyone you speak to, which means you'll decide to follow one person's advice and then change your mind if the next person you talk to has different ideas. Carry on like this and you'll end up feeling totally confused and bemused, as will everyone around you.

• *Tuesday 4 May* •

This is a super day for tackling financial matters and official paperwork, especially if it requires plenty of concentration on your part. You certainly know what you're doing at the moment and you'll be pleased with all the progress you make. This is also a good day for picking the brains of a financial wizard or talking to someone whose opinion you respect.

• *Wednesday 5 May* •

Take care because your self-esteem could easily take a battering today. Maybe someone is trying to make you feel demoralized, or is subtly undermining you. Of course, you may be helping the process along by putting yourself down or sabotaging all your efforts. It's a disheartening day but don't use it as an excuse to give yourself a really hard time.

• *Thursday 6 May* •

You're feeling much more positive than you were yesterday, making you determined to undo any damage you think you might have caused to your reputation or self-confidence. You could also receive a big pat on the back from a certain someone, which will help to restore your equilibrium and your faith in yourself.

• *Friday 7 May* •

Over the next few weeks you'll have a strong urge to enjoy yourself as much as possible, especially when you're with loved ones. Your libido will be much more active than usual, making you feel lusty and lascivious at times. If you're single, you might have a sexy fling with someone, but be careful not to confuse lust and love because that could end up breaking your tender heart.

• *Saturday 8 May* •

Oh dear! Someone close to your heart is being very remote and stand-offish this Saturday, making you wonder what you've done to upset them. Well, before you chew your fingernails down to the quick in anguish, let me reassure you that you probably haven't done anything at all and it's far more likely that this person's distant mood has nothing to do with you. It will soon pass.

• *Sunday 9 May* •

You hanker for social activity and gregarious settings today, and you'll feel rather cheated if you have to spend the day by yourself. It's certainly a super day for being with others because you'll find it so easy to hit it off with everyone you meet. A group or neighbourhood activity will be good fun and could introduce you to some interesting new contacts.

• *Monday 10 May* •

If life has been rather difficult with you-know-who recently, today is a marvellous opportunity to extend an olive branch and make your peace with them. You'll manage to say exactly the right thing at the right time, enabling you to create a harmonious and easy-going atmosphere in which you can both relax and enjoy one another's company.

• *Tuesday 11 May* •

Underlying tensions make this a rather tricky day, so take care. Maybe you're worried about certain secrets coming to light, or you're bothered about something that you daren't talk about. Be wary when discussing other people because you could accidentally let slip something that should really be left unsaid.

• *Wednesday 12 May* •

You're in a very restless and unsettled mood, making you easily bored. Ideally, you should keep switching from one activity to the next in order to keep your mind interested. If life threatens to get really boring you'll be tempted to liven things up by being a disruptive influence or dropping a bombshell. Can't you find more constructive ways of letting off steam?

• *Thursday 13 May* •

You've got plenty to say for yourself this Thursday and there may even be times when you barely draw breath! Although you're in such a chatty mood you won't be very popular if you completely dominate the conversation and don't allow anyone else to say more than two words at a time. This is especially likely if you're talking about matters that seem trivial to everyone else.

• *Friday 14 May* •

Watch out for big clashes with loved ones today, especially if the vexed question of money raises its ugly head. Maybe you'll object to the way you-know-who is flinging their cash around left, right and centre, or they're accusing you of being a spendthrift. You may also have to deal with someone who's being bossy, making you long to bring them down a peg or two.

• *Saturday 15 May* •

Life isn't much fun. You're feeling unloved and lonely, regardless of whether this is the true state of play or purely a figment of your imagination. You're taking problems very much to heart, making you extremely sensitive and attuned to the slightest hint of rejection or criticism. What's wrong, and how can you make things better?

• *Sunday 16 May* •

You'll be dashing around hither and thither over the next few weeks, and every now and then you'll wonder how on earth you're going to be able to find the time for everything you need to do. Yet somehow it will all get done, and you'll even manage to fit in some extra activities as well. It will be an especially good time to take off on short trips and weekend breaks.

• *Monday 17 May* •

A certain someone has a dynamic and exciting impact on you today. They're exuding so much sexual magnetism and charisma at the moment that they should carry a government health warning. It will be difficult to keep your hands off them, especially if your relationship is still in its early stages.

You're being driven by reckless urges, but should you give in to them or try to keep some control over them?

• *Tuesday 18 May* •

You're feeling distracted, vague and absent-minded, making it difficult to keep track of what you're supposed to be doing. It will be almost impossible to concentrate on anything for long because your mind will refuse to play ball, and instead will drift off in all sorts of directions. Yet you'll be brilliant at using your imagination and tuning in to your intuition.

• *Wednesday 19 May* •

You could meet some new people over the coming fortnight, so seize every chance to get out and about. This will also be an excellent period for improving the way you communicate with others, whether this means upgrading your mobile phone, signing up to the Internet, or making more of an effort to keep in touch with friends and family.

• *Thursday 20 May* •

Over the next few weeks you'll have a hankering to stay close to home whenever possible because this will make you feel safe and secure. You could even be inspired to do some DIY or decorating in order to make your nest feel more cosy or look more attractive. If you haven't seen various members of the clan for a long time you could be inspired to arrange a big reunion.

• *Friday 21 May* •

Your mind is racing and you're eager for interesting experiences and encounters. Your idea of heaven right now is to talk to someone who keeps you on the edge of your seat, or who has a radical way of looking at the world. You'll also enjoy doing things on the spur of the moment, especially if they seem rather wacky to everyone else.

• *Saturday 22 May* •

If you've been wondering when to come on strong to a certain person, tell them that you love them or break the ice with someone who might become a friend, do it today! You're ready to cast caution to the winds and to do whatever it is that you want, regardless of the consequences. Good luck, but make sure you know when to back down or protect yourself.

• *Sunday 23 May* •

This is the perfect day for doing as little as possible! If you try to start anything new this Sunday it will quickly go awry, so you may as well save yourself the frustration by not even attempting it. Instead, either carry on with projects that you've already begun or take the opportunity to put your feet up, read the Sunday papers and vegetate to your heart's content.

• *Monday 24 May* •

Someone has some brilliant ideas and they can't wait to tell you all about them. They're full of enthusiasm and excitement, and you'll soon feel equally positive. Take care if you're making promises to someone because you could soon get carried away, offering to do things that will turn out to be difficult or even impossible to fulfil.

• *Tuesday 25 May* •

It's hard to make much progress today because the odds are stacked against you. If you're relying on someone's co-operation you won't get it for some reason, and you may even suspect that they're deliberately trying to spike your guns. You also don't have as much energy as usual, which will slow you down and make you feel lethargic.

• *Wednesday 26 May* •

This is a wonderful day for taking care of the domestic chores, and for enjoying yourself in the process. You'll get a strong sense of satisfaction from pottering around at home or looking after your loved ones. You'll also be pleased with the progress you make at work, and with the happy atmosphere between you and your colleagues.

• *Thursday 27 May* •

It won't take much to make you feel as though you're being restricted and suffocated by other people's emotional needs today, and your immediate reaction will be to break away from them. You're also very sensitive to any hint of boredom or predictability, and at the first whiff of tedium you'll do your best to liven things up. As a result, this will be a disruptive day.

• *Friday 28 May* •

Be very careful about who and what you believe this Friday. Confusion and deception are rife, so this is a very bad day for making important decisions or reaching agreements. Unfortunately, it seems that someone may not be telling you the truth, or perhaps you're refusing to acknowledge certain facts and are therefore doing a good job of pulling the wool over your own eyes.

• *Saturday 29 May* •

If you're busy trying to find a new home or organize your moving arrangements, this will be a very productive and satisfying day. People are working with you rather than against you, so you'll make lots of progress and will be pleased with what develops. If you're involved in any form of property deal now you should make sure you stick within your budget.

• *Sunday 30 May* •

A loved one is fiercely territorial today and they won't like it if they think you're drifting away from them or not doing what they want. A row will be almost inevitable, but look on it as a chance to clear the air and get certain things off your chest. All the same, it won't help if you start to dredge up long-dead grievances, so make sure you stick to the relevant facts.

• *Monday 31 May* •

If you're usually a cautious Piscean you'll have a lot of fun today because you'll be eager to take risks and push yourself further than usual. However, if you're usually rather reckless, you could be tempted to go completely over the top now unless you manage to keep a firm grip on yourself. Moderation is the key to success this Monday!

JUNE AT A GLANCE

Love	♥ ♥ ♥ ♥ ♥
Money	£ $
Career	💻 💻 💻
Health	☼ ☼ ☼

• *Tuesday 1 June* •

It's horribly easy to get caught up in nit-picking and hair-splitting today, especially if you disagree with someone. You'll spend ages correcting each other and disputing the facts, none of which will get you very far. You're also easily swayed by other people's opinions right now, making it very difficult to make up your mind about anything.

• *Wednesday 2 June* •

The thought of having to bow down to convention or limitations is enough to make you want to scream right now, and you'll do your utmost to rebel in any way you can. Be careful about this because you could easily get on the wrong side of someone who has power or authority over you. It will feel as though you're battling with forces that want to keep you under control, and you won't like it one bit.

• *Thursday 3 June* •

Relationships are very fraught right now and you may even get the distinct impression that you're heading for a major showdown with someone. Although this feels like a crisis, don't let a sense of panic or desperation push you into decisions that you would normally steer clear of. You may think you've reached the end of the road with a particular situation or person but this isn't necessarily a good reason to go off the deep end and make drastic decisions. Take care!

• *Friday 4 June* •

Even if you feel frazzled by events, you get some light relief today, so make the most of it. This is a wonderful opportunity to get together with people who always make you laugh or who help you to forget about your current troubles. It's also a marvellous day for linking up with kindred spirits or for immersing yourself in a favourite hobby.

• *Saturday 5 June* •

Your thoughts will be drawn back to the past over the next fortnight, putting you in a reflective and rather nostalgic mood at times. This is a great chance to look through your old photos, letters and other keepsakes, and also to talk about the past with people who shared it with you. But don't forget that you're living in the present!

• *Sunday 6 June* •

It's delightfully easy to get on well with loved ones today, thanks to the harmonious and accepting atmosphere between you. You're ready to take others as you find them, and even to overlook some of their more irritating traits. It's also a day to confide in people and to listen when they confide in you.

• *Monday 7 June* •

You're feeling nicely relaxed and positive, which will help you to take the day's events in your stride. Mind you, you'll prefer it if you can have a low-key and reflective day rather than get involved in a lot of noise and bustle. It's a super day for setting aside the time to do some meditation or creative visualization, and you'll really feel the benefits.

• *Tuesday 8 June* •

A loved one is feeling extremely chatty, as you'll soon discover when they virtually talk your ears off. You won't mind, unless you've got something important to say and can't squeeze a word in edgeways. Nevertheless, this is a great day for having a family pow-wow in which everyone gets the chance to have their say about forthcoming plans and arrangements.

• *Wednesday 9 June* •

You're anxious to prove that you're a person in your own right rather than part of a family unit, so you'll grab every chance you can find to assert your own individuality. You may even want to fly in the face of convention or family rules in order to get your point across or to make certain people sit up and take notice. It's important to know how far you can push this without alienating everyone around you.

• *Thursday 10 June* •

This is a great day for making domestic plans, provided that you know where to draw the line. But if you allow your imagination to run wild, you'll come up with ideas that are far too ambitious ever to see the light of day and which will turn out to be a complete waste of time. You may also have to listen to someone who's apparently completely infatuated with the sound of their own voice.

• *Friday 11 June* •

It's difficult to keep the peace with people in authority at the moment and this is another day when tension is never far away. Maybe someone is laying down the law and expecting you to do exactly what they tell you, or perhaps you're the one who's insisting on being in control. Take care, because either extreme will lead to trouble. You need to find some sort of happy medium.

• *Saturday 12 June* •

In true Piscean style, you long to bury your head in the sand and retreat from harsh reality into a world of your own. The more difficult life is right now, the more you'll long for some escapism. That's fine, provided that you're prepared to face facts again soon. In the meantime, a loved one will offer you tremendous consolation and affection, much to your delight and gratitude.

• *Sunday 13 June* •

Once again you're on the hunt for as much escapism as possible. Today you might find it by disappearing into a delicious nostalgic daydream or by becoming completely absorbed in a romantic film. Speaking of romance, someone is being very flattering and loving, but beware of only hearing what you want to hear in what they're saying.

• *Monday 14 June* •

It's a terrific day for getting things done without having to make too much effort. People are being co-operative and helpful, you know what you're doing, and life flows along at a nice, steady pace. If you're busy organizing a forthcoming social event, this is a good day to chase up any loose ends and make sure that everything is under control.

• *Tuesday 15 June* •

This is a magnificent day for getting to the bottom of things and finding out what's really going on. You'll want to leave no stone unturned in your efforts to get at the truth, which could cause problems if you start to interfere in things that are none of your business. Beware of a tendency to stick your nose in where it's not wanted or to become obsessive about someone or something: this will make you very unpopular.

• *Wednesday 16 June* •

Surround yourself with loved ones. It will do you good to be with people who know you inside out, and with whom you feel safe and comfortable. These might be your nearest and dearest, or they could be close friends who are family in all but name. If you fancy spending some money, you'll enjoy buying items for your home or garden.

• *Thursday 17 June* •

Today's New Moon will have an energizing and revitalizing effect on your domestic life during the coming fortnight. This might be your cue to move house or to do up your existing home, especially if you've been toying with the idea for ages but haven't done anything concrete about it. There could also be an addition to the family circle in the near future.

• *Friday 18 June* •

It's difficult to get much done today because certain people keep interrupting you. Maybe they're desperate for a chat so they gas away for hours, or they follow you around like a devoted puppy dog. There will be lots of comings and goings on the home front, with plenty of visitors or phone calls. It will be good fun, provided that you don't have anything more urgent to attend to.

• *Saturday 19 June* •

Pleasure is your number one priority this Saturday and you'll find any excuse to let your hair down. Ideally, you should be doing some lavish entertaining, visiting close friends or doing something else that's equally convivial. If you're going out on a hot date with you-know-who, try to keep your high expectations under control; if you don't, you'll be sorely disappointed by reality.

• *Sunday 20 June* •

A loved one is a real handful today. They're playful, aggressive and moody, and you've got your work cut out in trying to cope with them. You need to find a constructive outlet for your abundant nervous energy or you'll become equally irascible and edgy. Ideally, you should do something physical, such as going for a brisk walk or having a session in the gym.

• *Monday 21 June* •

Love and laughter will never be far away during the coming month, so there will be plenty to look forward to. This will be one of the highlights of your year, so make the most of it whenever you get the chance. Surround yourself with loved ones, do things that make you feel carefree and light-hearted, and concentrate on expressing your true self at every opportunity.

• *Tuesday 22 June* •

Expect the unexpected and you won't be disappointed! It's the sort of day in which anything can and will happen, and you might also hear some very interesting news. Be prepared to be flexible if your plans change at the last minute, and also to be spontaneous and open-minded. Acting on hunches could turn out to be a very clever move now, too.

• *Wednesday 23 June* •

You're going to be kept very busy over the next few weeks, especially where your work is concerned. You might have to put in more hours than usual, perhaps because you're covering for someone else or are extra busy with your own tasks. You'll want to receive plenty of recognition for all this, but whether you get it is another matter.

• *Thursday 24 June* •

Someone is being highly dogmatic and stubborn today, and they want to call the shots at every opportunity. They're also being rather controlling, so you feel that you're their puppet and you have to dance to their tune. Will you like this? Of course not, and you'll make your objections known at the first opportunity.

• *Friday 25 June* •

Friends and loved ones are full of great suggestions today, and you'll be tempted to follow up as many as possible. For instance, someone might suggest going out on the razzle when you'd decided to have an early night, and so you'll change your plans to fit in with theirs. It will be a very enjoyable day but it could work out expensive, so be warned.

• *Saturday 26 June* •

Someone is in an odd mood. They're being critical and rather scratchy, so you feel that you ought to pussyfoot around them in order to keep them sweet. However, such pacifying tactics will soon lose their appeal and you may even start to engineer situations in such a way that they inevitably lead to a row, giving you a chance to let off steam and stamp your feet.

• *Sunday 27 June* •

Try not to take a loved one's words too much to heart today. They're withdrawn, unfriendly or distant, making you wonder what on earth you've done to upset them. They may also be rather hard on you, perhaps by pointing out some of your faults or ticking you off about something. Turn the tables by asking them what's wrong, because something is obviously troubling them.

• *Monday 28 June* •

You have a strong need to express yourself today and to prove that you're an individual in your own right. You don't want to be neatly filed away in a pigeon-hole; instead, you want people to recognize that you're a unique human being. You're at your most dazzling and engaging right now, and your sparkling personality will attract plenty of admirers.

• *Tuesday 29 June* •

This is a wonderful day for planning something that you can look forward to. That might be a social event at the weekend, a visit to a friend or your next holiday. Whatever it is, it will be good to know that it's coming up on the horizon. Your brain is working really well now so give it plenty of exercise, especially if that means trying your luck at puzzles, competitions or quizzes.

• *Wednesday 30 June* •

One of the women in your life needs plenty of love and attention today, or she'll make a bit of a fuss. Even a short phone call or a brief visit will do the trick, and will help to avoid her feeling ignored or left out. If you're at work it won't hurt to gently butter up a boss or authority figure, provided that you do it with subtlety and tact.

JULY AT A GLANCE

Love	♥ ♥ ♥ ♥ ♥
Money	£ $
Career	💻 💻 💻 💻 💻
Health	☼ ☼ ☼ ☼ ☼

• *Thursday 1 July* •

You're in a very ambitious and go-getting frame of mind today, and you don't want to mess around in any way. In fact, you're extremely eager to cut to the chase and to get on with whatever requires your attention, even if this causes problems in other areas of your life. This is a super day for concentrating on your goals, but it's important to keep them in perspective.

• *Friday 2 July* •

Today's Full Moon will have a dramatic impact on some of your friendships during the next two weeks. If things have been dicey with someone recently, matters will soon come to a head. This isn't necessarily a bad thing because it might help you to sort out a tricky situation and then get it back on track. You might even find that talking through your differences helps to bring you closer together.

• *Saturday 3 July* •

Take care because it's one of those days in which it's easy to let your emotions get the better of you, making you sensitive and easily hurt. You might read too much into a situation, so that it assumes monumental importance, or your damaged feelings might make you lash out at other people in an effort to get your own back. Try to keep calm and not get all stirred up about things that don't really matter.

• *Sunday 4 July* •

Put on your thinking cap over the next couple of weeks because this will be a marvellous opportunity to make progress at work. That might mean getting on with a pile of paperwork that's been waiting your attention for ages, or finally deciding to look for a better job. It will also be a great chance to take part in discussions and meetings, because you'll have plenty to say.

• *Monday 5 July* •

Relationships are a real joy today, thanks to the sunny disposition of certain people and your determination to have as much fun as possible. Do yourself a favour and get together with friends and loved ones whenever you have the chance, even if this means rearranging your plans and postponing various chores until later in the week. You aren't in the mood for them anyway!

• *Tuesday 6 July* •

This is another gloriously happy and easy-going day, when once again you'll get a lot of pleasure from being with some of your favourite people. It's also a super day for expressing yourself through some of your abundant artistic talents, whether you're creating something yourself or admiring someone else's efforts.

• *Wednesday 7 July* •

Dealings with a certain someone are tricky to say the least today. They're in a serious and rather bossy mood, making it difficult to talk to them for long without getting embroiled in a battle of wills. Before you know where you are, you'll be as desperate as they are to gain control of the conversation and you won't give this up easily. Take care!

• *Thursday 8 July* •

You're feeling slightly distant and at one step removed from loved ones today, and you'll probably be better off if you can be left to your own devices for a short while. Try not to give anyone the impression that you've gone off them or that you're displeased with them, simply because you've withdrawn your attention from them for a short while. They may need some reassurance on this score.

• *Friday 9 July* •

Money causes a few skirmishes between you and a special person today. Maybe you think they're throwing their cash away on something frivolous, or they think they've got the right to tick you off about your spending habits. If you read between the lines you may realize that something bigger is going on here, and that you're actually involved in a dispute about someone's need to go their own way and someone else's need to keep control of them.

• *Saturday 10 July* •

It will be almost impossible to guard your tongue and not let it run away with you today, which will make life rather tricky at times. That's because you'll quickly get heated and will then say things that are unwise, unhelpful or just plain rude. Yes, you! This is most likely to happen if you're in a tearing hurry or are feeling hard-done-by and taken for granted. You need to calm down!

• *Sunday 11 July* •

Thank goodness you're being much more tactful and considerate today, which makes a big change from yesterday's tendency to say the wrong thing at the wrong time. If you need to do some apologizing, get it out of the way sooner rather than later, so you can put the whole episode behind you with a clear conscience. By the way, this is also a super day for having a family discussion.

• *Monday 12 July* •

Don't start any new projects today unless you want them to fizzle out or you enjoy wasting your time on hopeless causes. This is one of those trying days when things don't go according to plan, especially if you're putting them into action for the first time. There could also be some crossed wires when talking to others, so be careful not to mislead anyone or give the wrong impression.

• *Tuesday 13 July* •

It's difficult to keep your mind on anything for long today. You're feeling distracted and easily confused, so you could easily misinterpret what others are telling you or simply not listen to them in the first place. Be very careful if you're supposed to be concentrating on something important: that will be virtually impossible this Tuesday, unless it involves your imagination.

• *Wednesday 14 July* •

A certain person is brimming with enthusiasm about something and they're very keen for you to join in. Do you really want to, or are you doing it just to be polite? Be wary of pretending too much because this could raise their hopes and eventually lead to a lot of disappointment and bad feeling. Far better to be honest now than have to backtrack at a later date.

• *Thursday 15 July* •

Life is full of excitement today, with plenty of unexpected events to keep you on your toes. Loved ones will be especially unpredictable, although this will be nothing to worry about. Instead, someone might arrange a wonderful treat for you, or make a suggestion that has you jumping up and down for joy. You might also have an enjoyable flirtation with a certain someone. It seems harmless on the surface, but how does it feel deep down?

• *Friday 16 July* •

You're at your most sensitive and impressionable today, making you want to shy away from anyone who's being crass or difficult. You need to be surrounded by people you can trust and who like you, or you'll soon get rather uncomfortable. Romance may not be very far away, so dim the lights, play some seductive music and gaze into the eyes of you-know-who.

• *Saturday 17 July* •

Today's New Moon promises to bring you lots of happiness and laughter over the coming fortnight. This is the perfect excuse to spend as much time as possible with some of your favourite people, and also to tell them how much they mean to you. You're at your most demonstrative and affectionate right now, and it will give you real pleasure to dispense hugs and kisses in all directions. Everyone else will be thrilled, too!

• *Sunday 18 July* •

This is a perfect day for getting on with mundane chores. They're exactly what you're in the mood for, partly because you'll take comfort from doing something so everyday and ordinary, and partly because you'll be pleased to have ticked various things off your list of things to do. At some point you may have to do your Florence Nightingale act with someone who isn't well.

• *Monday 19 July* •

Carry on from yesterday and continue to work on day-to-day tasks and projects. This is an especially good day for doing some cleaning or tidying up, particularly if you're fed up with looking at things that are really only gathering dust at the moment. Get a big bin bag and throw out anything that's cluttering up your living space or working environment.

• *Tuesday 20 July* •

You're full of love and affection today, and it's got to come out one way or the other. If a special person isn't around at the moment, give them a ring or send them a card so they know you're thinking about them. You're feeling sociable, so a great way to use today's loving energies would be to invite some friends round to your place and give them a rip-roaring time.

• *Wednesday 21 July* •

The more you've been trying to ignore your feelings about a certain someone recently, the more control they'll exert over you this Wednesday. This means that you'll soon be at the mercy of some powerful and compulsive emotions, which could make you behave in ways that you wouldn't normally dream of. Do your best to keep things in proportion and not to give in to obsessive thoughts.

• *Thursday 22 July* •

The coming four weeks will be a busy time for you at work, so be prepared to put in more hours than usual or to have more on your agenda. Yet you won't want to skimp on anything or cut corners because you'll take great pride in doing tasks to the best of your ability. This will also be a good opportunity to pay more attention to your health and general well-being.

• *Friday 23 July* •

You're very tuned in to other people today and the more you care about them, the greater the psychic connection you'll have with them now. You may even know what they're thinking without them having to say anything, but take care not to make gigantic assumptions about them that are based more on wishful thinking than on your instincts.

• *Saturday 24 July* •

If you're thinking of going shopping today you'll really enjoy browsing around interior design and food shops. You'll love seeing what's on offer and wondering whether items would look good in your home. Ideally, you should take someone special with you to keep you company, and also to restrain you from any wild indulgences that suddenly sweep over you.

• *Sunday 25 July* •

Communications are even more important than usual over the next few weeks, because you'll get the opportunity to lay your cards on the table and say exactly what you think. This will be far more productive than pussyfooting around or hoping to say what you assume others want to hear. This could cause ructions at the time but you must be honest and straightforward.

• *Monday 26 July* •

Broaden your experience of life in some way today. This might mean burying your nose in a book that teaches you something new, talking to someone whose conversation grips you like a vice or strolling around somewhere that you've always wanted to visit. Right now you're able to absorb information almost without realizing it, so keep your mind open and soak up some knowledge.

• *Tuesday 27 July* •

Your relationships with colleagues and family members go well today, and it's easy to keep on the right side of them. You're even able to stick your neck out quite a long way without incurring any problems, leading to a lively and stimulating atmosphere. If you've currently got the hots for someone at work, you'll be very tempted to make a big play for them now. Good luck!

• *Wednesday 28 July* •

Someone has allowed their power or position to go to their head this Wednesday, making them tolerable only in small doses. Unfortunately, you may have to spend more time with them than you'd like, especially if they happen to be your boss or an older relative. Let their domineering ways wash over you, leaving you unaffected and unmoved. It's the only way to cope.

• *Thursday 29 July* •

A friend really brightens up your day today, especially if they suddenly appear out of the blue and mean that you have to change all your plans. Don't worry because this will be great fun, and the new arrangements will be much more enjoyable than the old ones. It's also a good day to take part in a group activity, although it will involve a few surprises or unexpected developments.

• *Friday 30 July* •

Don't panic! A certain someone is keeping their distance, whether physically or emotionally, and it feels really scary. However, it's unlikely to be as serious or long lasting as you imagine, so try not to read anything sinister into the situation. Perhaps this person simply needs some time to themselves, or maybe they're miserable and need you to put your arms around them and make them feel better.

• *Saturday 31 July* •

Today's Full Moon is urging you to sort out anything that's been bothering you recently, before it gets any worse or starts to cause you sleepless nights. Being a Piscean means you're very good at procrastinating and turning a blind eye to anything unpleasant, but during the coming fortnight you've got to face up to what's going on in your life and take constructive action over it. Start right now!

AUGUST AT A GLANCE

Love	♥ ♥ ♥ ♥ ♥
Money	£ $
Career	💻 💻 💻 💻 💻
Health	☼ ☼ ☼ ☼ ☼

• *Sunday 1 August* •

Someone is being really outspoken, and possibly even shocking, today. They seem to be deliberately going out of their way to say things that cause a commotion or bring them plenty of attention. Now, the big question is whether you're behaving in the same way, in which case you need to get a grip before you say something that will land you in boiling hot water. What's up with you, anyway?

• *Monday 2 August* •

Whether or not you were responsible for yesterday's ructions, you're in a very restless and agitated state today. It's hard to settle down to anything for long, and when you do you'll quickly get bored and want to move on to something else. You have excess nervous energy right now and need to find some constructive outlets for it; otherwise it could make you do something reckless or shocking.

• *Tuesday 3 August* •

Relationships are much more easy-going and enjoyable today, thank goodness. Everyone seems to be going out of their way to be friendly, and you're also at your chummiest. It's a wonderful excuse to get together with someone who always makes you laugh, because life will look very different after you've had a good giggle together.

• *Wednesday 4 August* •

A woman in your life needs plenty of love and attention today, or she'll make her displeasure known. Even if you're busy with other things, it will be much better to give her what she wants than to ignore her and then have to patch things up later on. A quick hug, a phone call or a five-minute chat will do the trick if you can't spare the time for anything else at the moment.

• *Thursday 5 August* •

This is a super day for getting on with whichever chores are currently top of your list of priorities. It will be good to know that you're doing something about them, and you'll also take pride in doing them to the best of your ability. The atmosphere between you and a colleague is reassuring and enjoyable, so you'll do very good work together.

• *Friday 6 August* •

Someone is gripped by the need to make some radical and dramatic changes, but things aren't going their way. Maybe you're opposing their proposals and are prepared to resist them to the bitter end. If you're the one who's trying to introduce these changes, it's essential to consider the other people involved and not ride roughshod over their feelings, even if that means scaling down your plans.

• *Saturday 7 August* •

The next four weeks promise to be a glorious time for your love life. This might mean a really wonderful interlude with you-know-who, in which you fall in love with each other all over again, or someone new might enter your life. Or you might simply have a marvellously happy time with loved ones, friends and children, knowing that you all cherish one another's company. Fab, fab, fab!

• *Sunday 8 August* •

If you've been wondering when would be a good time to have a word with a certain person, do it today. You're in an easygoing and positive mood, making it easy for you to hit it off with everyone you meet. You'll also enjoy getting out and about at some point, so maybe this would be a good opportunity to drop in on a neighbour or venture a little further afield and have a day out.

• *Monday 9 August* •

You could hear some uncomfortable truths about yourself today, so be prepared not to like everything you're told. Although your instincts may tell you to deny what you're hearing, it would be far better to listen carefully. There may be a lot of truth in what you're told, even if you don't like to admit it to yourself.

• *Tuesday 10 August* •

Some of your relationships will be rather fraught between now and late September, thanks to a sudden inability on your part to compromise and allow others to go their own way. You want to call the shots, and to have a lot of control over partners, even if this drives them round the bend with irritation. So expect some heated encounters unless you can tone things down a little.

• *Wednesday 11 August* •

Even though some of your relationships will be tricky over the next few weeks, you see no signs of that today. Instead, you're able to enjoy a wonderfully affectionate and happy rapport with some of the special people in your life. Make the most of it while it lasts! It's also a super day to do something creative, such as sewing, dancing or painting.

• *Thursday 12 August* •

You have a lot of authority and self-command today, so you'll create a really good impression if you're taking charge of a group of people or doing something important at work. It's even better if you're taking part in an important meeting or job interview, because it will be obvious that you know exactly what you're doing.

• *Friday 13 August* •

Love takes you by surprise today. It might just knock your socks off, so stand by for some interesting encounters. There's even a chance that you could meet someone new and be completely smitten by them, or become involved in a hectic flirtation which leaves you wondering what's going to happen next. It's certainly going to be a fun-filled and exciting day!

• *Saturday 14 August* •

If you spend too much time alone today you'll soon feel as though something crucial is missing from your life, and you'll be right. It will be people who are missing, because this isn't a day for being by yourself if you can possibly help it. However, you may have to fight against a slight tendency to cling to others, or to seem too dependent on them.

• *Sunday 15 August* •

You're blessed with a great deal of tact and diplomacy today, so put it to good use. It's an ideal day to smooth over any problems that have emerged with a certain person recently, and you may even manage to eradicate them completely now simply by choosing your words carefully and, if necessary, admitting that you were in the wrong.

• *Monday 16 August* •

Your emotional, physical and spiritual welfare are highlighted by today's New Moon, so concentrate on them as much as possible during the next two weeks. Maybe you're involved in a situation that is making you feel ill, or draining your energy, and you now need to do something about it. This will also be a good time to begin a new health regime.

• *Tuesday 17 August* •

You're in a very realistic and sensible mood today, yet you won't be so wedded to common sense that you become stuffy or hidebound. Instead, you're able to combine a practical approach with an ability to look on the bright side of things and be positive about your future prospects. A relationship will flourish as a result of your marvellous attitude.

• *Wednesday 18 August* •

It won't take much to get you rather hot under the collar today, which will lead to a tendency to make unfortunate comments in the heat of the moment. Your mouth is working faster than your brain right now, so watch out or it will have some disastrous consequences. Even so, you may say things on the spur of the moment that need to be said, even if you do drop a brick in the process.

• *Thursday 19 August* •

Someone is giving you far too much information today, making it very difficult to process what you're being told. Maybe this person is barely pausing for breath, so everything comes out in a never-ending stream of consciousness. You'll also encounter someone who's making outrageous comments that are designed to wind you up. Will you rise to the bait or manage to remain cool, calm and collected?

• *Friday 20 August* •

The emotional temperature is below par today, leaving you feeling chilly and rather sorry for yourself. Maybe a loved one is annoyed with you for some reason and is taking it out on you by withdrawing their affection or being rather aloof. Yet you may also be sending out signals that make others want to retreat in self-defence, even if you aren't aware of what you're doing.

• *Saturday 21 August* •

It's a good day for taking care of everyday chores and practical tasks, in order to ensure that your life will run as smoothly as possible. You might want to do some filing, so that you can lay your hands on important paperwork whenever you need it instead of scrabbling around in drawers while being assailed by waves of panic. So get organized, and feel proud of yourself for doing so!

• *Sunday 22 August* •

Your sense of identity will be strongly coloured by the state of your relationships over the next four weeks. If you feel lonely or on the shelf, you'll think that this reflects badly on you and you'll want to do something about it. It will certainly be an excellent time for any sort of team work, because you'll do your utmost to make sure you pull your weight.

• *Monday 23 August* •

Tensions are building up between you and a certain person today, leading to some tricky moments. If you've been desperately trying to swallow your irritation with this person, that could go by the wayside now when you finally erupt in a big show of anger. It will certainly be better to blow your top than to simmer any longer, but don't let things get out of control.

• *Tuesday 24 August* •

You need to take things gently today, especially if you're expected to get through a stack of work. It isn't what you're in the mood for, and you may struggle to concentrate after a while. It will help to have plenty of short breaks by yourself, so you can recharge your batteries and enjoy a little peace and quiet before re-entering the fray.

• *Wednesday 25 August* •

Take care of yourself during the next three weeks because you'll have a distinct tendency to skimp on your food and sleep. You may have so much work to do that it's difficult to find time for much else, but allowing your energy to run down will eventually make you less efficient and will also mean that everything takes longer than it should.

• *Thursday 26 August* •

You're in a very dynamic mood today, so you're approaching everything with plenty of zip and enthusiasm. It's an especially good day for getting other people involved in your own projects because you'll soon be able to advertise the merits of what you're doing. However, it's important that you know when to try to persuade someone to do what you want and when it would be better to hold back and not push them any further.

• *Friday 27 August* •

You need to prove that you're an individual in your own right today, and you won't like it one bit if someone is trying to fit you into a neat stereotype or make you toe the line when you don't want to. You may even feel compelled to do something reckless or drastic in order to get your point across, but do this only if you've exhausted every other avenue without getting anywhere.

• *Saturday 28 August* •

You're in a very dreamy and preoccupied mood this Saturday, so that you seem to be wandering around in a world of your own. Ideally, you should take the day off so you can relax in peace without having to worry about making mistakes or giving people the wrong impression, because both of these are easily done right now. Try to steer clear of alcohol– it will only make you feel worse.

• *Sunday 29 August* •

It's horribly easy to get caught up in tiny details today, so that you eventually lose sight of the bigger picture and become obsessed with the minutiae of life instead. This is especially likely if you're tackling some paperwork or are doing something that should have been finished a long time ago and which you now feel guilty about.

• *Monday 30 August* •

Today's Full Moon is one of the most important of the year for you because it's encouraging you to cut out the dross from your personal life, whether this is a situation that's gone on for too long, a relationship that no longer has anything to offer you or a habit that you need to kick. Grit your teeth and start making changes that you know are long overdue. They'll lead to a new you.

• *Tuesday 31 August* •

Love relationships are rather low-key today, and might even be hard work, but they are worth persevering with because the results will be great. For instance, you might go through a sticky patch with your beloved, but if you have the guts to sort it out you'll both develop a greater understanding of what makes your relationship tick and the level of stress that it can endure.

SEPTEMBER AT A GLANCE

Love	♥ ♥ ♥ ♥
Money	£ $ £ $ £
Career	💻 💻 💻
Health	☼ ☼ ☼

• *Wednesday 1 September* •

Do yourself a favour and devote some time this Wednesday to activities that make your world go round. For instance, you might get busy with a favourite occupation or make a point of seeing one of the most important people in your life. This is definitely a day for pampering yourself whenever you get the chance, even if all you can do is buy yourself a bar of chocolate or have a long soak in the bath. It's quality rather than quantity that counts now!

• *Thursday 2 September* •

This promises to be one of the nicest days in the whole of September, especially if you can be with some of your nearest and dearest. You're feeling extremely sociable and outgoing, so you'll get on well with everyone you meet, but you'll be happiest when you're with some of your favourite people. A close relationship will go wonderfully well, and you could hear something that's so sweet or loving that you'll be blushing for hours to come.

• *Friday 3 September* •

You're still in a very gregarious mood, so enjoy it while it lasts. This is a super day for any form of socializing, whether it's business or pleasure, because you've got the happy knack of being able to bring out the best in other people and make them feel that you're genuinely interested in them. Play your cards right and you could be a big hit with a certain someone now.

• *Saturday 4 September* •

Today is a super day because you're blessed with abundant energy, helping you to cope with whatever comes your way. You're in quite a fiery and powerful mood, making you the centre of attention for the best possible reasons. If you've been waiting for the right time to talk someone into seeing things your way, you stand an excellent chance of doing so today.

• *Sunday 5 September* •

Be careful, especially if you're at home, because you could easily become accident-prone this Sunday. This is especially likely to happen if you're suffering from a lot of pent-up nervous energy that can't be released, or if you have to cope with a series of unexpected events that throw you for a loop and leave you feeling jittery. Do your best to keep calm.

• *Monday 6 September* •

Between now and early October you'll want to give service with a smile at every opportunity. This means that you'll take additional pride in your work, and also in your ability to get on well with colleagues and customers. There might even be some romantic activity with someone you meet in the course of your job or through some other everyday activity.

• *Tuesday 7 September* •

You're caught in the grip of powerful emotions today, particularly if problems from the past have reappeared or you're embroiled in a highly charged conflict with someone. Tread carefully because you'll be tempted to behave in compulsive or obsessive ways that will only make the situation worse. Stand up for yourself if needs be, but do it fairly and without being manipulative.

• *Wednesday 8 September* •

Do something on the spur of the moment today! Maybe you should ring up a friend and fix up a last-minute outing, or rearrange existing plans so you can do something more exciting. There could also be an unexpected but enjoyable connection with a certain person, perhaps when you bump into them by accident or they ring you out of the blue.

• *Thursday 9 September* •

Your relationships are running very smoothly today, because you're able to strike exactly the right note with other people and win them over. You'll get on well with virtually everyone you meet, whether they're total strangers or your best friends, and you'll certainly have a whale of a time if you're going out on the razzle or are being whisked off on a hot date.

• *Friday 10 September* •

Your relationship with a certain person grinds to a bad-tempered halt today, with both of you stubbornly sticking to your guns and refusing to acknowledge the other person's point of view. This situation will become even more critical if one of you sees it as a chance to assert your authority or even to crush the other one into submission. Don't do it, Pisces!

• *Saturday 11 September* •

What's wrong? You're feeling lacklustre, with a strong desire to retreat from the world. Maybe you're simply tired and could do with a break, or perhaps something is weighing on your mind and draining your energy. Try to steer clear of any food or drink that doesn't always agree with you because it will have quite a detrimental effect on you at the moment.

• *Sunday 12 September* •

Once again you're involved in a clash with a certain someone, and it will soon turn to stalemate if you aren't careful. Maybe they're exerting too much power over you and you're making your displeasure very obvious, or perhaps your relationship with them is going through major changes that are having a very stressful impact on you. Do your best, and keep plodding on.

• *Monday 13 September* •

You're speaking and thinking much more rapidly than usual. This could be really exciting, with lots of original and innovative ideas rushing through your mind. However, it may also mean that you're being rather too blunt for comfort because you aren't giving yourself enough time to think things through before blurting them out. So expect to see some shocked faces!

• *Tuesday 14 September* •

Your partnerships get a shot in the arm from today, and this happy state of affairs will continue for the next two weeks. This might be your cue to salvage a relationship that's in trouble at the moment by adopting a different strategy towards it, or by levelling with the person concerned about your feelings for them. A few miracles might happen as a result of your actions.

• *Wednesday 15 September* •

Go carefully when handling partners and associates today because you're feeling rather impatient and hasty, and you could easily get on the wrong side of them by provoking them in some way. You might also have a showdown with someone who's been irritating the life out of you recently and who you think is long overdue for a piece of your mind. Put your tin hat on!

• *Thursday 16 September* •

A great wave of sentiment washes over you this Thursday, making you highly emotional and very tuned in to your surroundings. Your antennae are working overtime, enabling you to pick up undercurrents and know intuitively what's going on with the people around you. Trust your instincts, because they'll guide you in the right direction.

• *Friday 17 September* •

A loved one is a towering support today, much to your delight. It's obvious that they're behind you all the way, and you're really grateful to them for their help. So why not say so? This is also a marvellous day to build bridges with someone if you've fallen out with them recently, and to start to repair your relationship piece by piece.

• *Saturday 18 September* •

You're wandering around in a fog today, making it almost impossible to see what's right in front of your eyes. This is especially true when it comes to your relationships with certain people in your life, because right now you're busy ignoring some unpleasant facts that are staring you in the face. OK, ignore them today if you must, but you'll have to acknowledge them soon.

• *Sunday 19 September* •

If you haven't heard recently from a friend or relative who lives a long way away, or even overseas, this is a good day for making contact with them again. They'll be thrilled to hear from you, and they might even be so chuffed that they invite you to visit them. If you can spare the time you'll enjoy a jaunt to a place that you've never seen before, especially if it's steeped in atmosphere.

• *Monday 20 September* •

Someone's favourite occupation today seems to be splitting hairs, and they're doing it with great precision. So much precision, in fact, that your face is rigid with suppressed yawns and you'll soon want to scream. However, the sad fact is that you may be equally pedantic and nit-picking right now, even if you don't realize it, particularly when it comes to red tape.

• *Tuesday 21 September* •

Your relationship with a certain someone goes through a renaissance today, and becomes even better than ever. You might spend all your time chortling with laughter, or discover that you have even more in common than you first thought. If you meet someone new now, they'll have an uplifting and exuberant impact on your life.

• *Wednesday 22 September* •

You have a strong desire to get to the truth today, which means you'll dig away at the facts until you find what you're looking for. This will make you extremely persistent, possibly even to the point of rudeness if you end up cross-examining someone or demanding that they give you the answers you're looking for.

• *Thursday 23 September* •

This is one of those delightful days when getting on well with other people is as easy as falling off a log. You're at your most charming and outgoing right now, so don't be surprised if you have everyone eating out of your hand before too long. And who can blame them when you're in this sort of mood? The positive reaction you get from everyone will do wonders for your self-confidence, especially if a certain someone only has eyes for you. It's great!

• *Friday 24 September* •

If a new relationship gets off the ground now it will always feel very intense and powerful, almost as though you're connected by a strong magnetic attraction. Before too long, you'll also realize that you were fated to meet for some reason, and that you'll both get a tremendous amount out of being together. This applies whether you're lovers, friends, colleagues or family.

• *Saturday 25 September* •

Your close relationships start to undergo a wonderful transformation from today, and over the next twelve months they'll blossom in all sorts of enriching and rewarding ways. There could also be more money on the horizon, whether your own earning power increases or you benefit from the largesse of some of the people in your life.

• *Sunday 26 September* •

You're talking a lot of sense today, particularly when it comes to discussions with loved ones. You're taking a very practical approach without losing either your sense of fun or your sense of humour. It's an especially good day for taking part in a discussion or serious conversation in which you're prepared to speak from the heart and say what you think.

• *Monday 27 September* •

Turn your attention to your finances because this is a brilliant day for boosting your income through some clever moves. You might decide to invest some spare cash for a rainy day, or you could strike lucky when a windfall lands at your feet. You're feeling slightly daring, but don't let this turn to recklessness and make you take gambles that you can't afford to lose.

• *Tuesday 28 September* •

The coming fortnight provides an excellent opportunity to get your money matters in order, and to pay particular attention to your everyday finances. For instance, you should go through bank and credit card statements in case they contain mistakes, and also pay any overdue bills before they lead to trouble. If you've been overspending this will be a good chance to cut back on your outgoings.

• *Wednesday 29 September* •

You're rather outspoken this Wednesday, as you're tending to open your mouth and say the first thing that comes into your head. This could lead to some tricky moments if you get excited or het up, as you'll then have an unerring ability to say the wrong thing. Try to curb your worst excesses and, if in doubt, keep quiet!

• *Thursday 30 September* •

Money, or the lack of it, is putting a crimp in your day. Maybe you've just received a hefty bill or a depressing bank statement, and you're feeling flattened and miserable as a result. Or perhaps you're realizing that an enjoyable trip or social event will have to be curtailed or even cancelled because it's going to cost too much money. Things seem bleak at the moment but they're unlikely to be as grim as you think, so take heart.

OCTOBER AT A GLANCE

Love	♥ ♥ ♥
Money	£ $ £ $ £
Career	💻 💻 💻
Health	☼ ☼ ☼

• *Friday 1 October* •

This is one of those difficult days when you live up to your sign's reputation for being distracted and absent-minded. Try as you might to marshal your thoughts and make them obey you, they'll keep skittering off in all sorts of different directions like naughty children, leaving you lost for words or wondering what you'd been thinking about before you were so rudely interrupted.

• *Saturday 2 October* •

Money! That's the main theme this Saturday because it's burning a great big hole in your pocket. You may not even want to buy anything in particular but you'll enjoy the whole performance of choosing something, paying for it and then taking it home in a swish carrier bag. It almost goes without saying that you should restrain yourself if you're supposed to be saving money rather than spending it at the moment.

• *Sunday 3 October* •

If a relationship has been languishing in the doldrums recently it gets a helping hand from today until late in the month. This will be a good opportunity for you to reach a compromise with someone if you've fallen out with them recently, or to make more of an effort to understand what has upset them and how you can make amends.

• *Monday 4 October* •

Take it easy today or you'll get all steamed up about things that you'd usually take in your stride. You could become especially exasperated about the way someone is throwing their weight around or issuing orders left, right and centre. Mind you, you won't be immune from doing this yourself, even if you aren't aware of it, so monitor yourself carefully for signs of bossy behaviour.

• *Tuesday 5 October* •

You're at your most compassionate, understanding and forgiving today. You're prepared to overlook someone's recent misdemeanours because you're well aware that we all make mistakes and you think they deserve a second chance. This is all to the good, provided that you aren't allowing yourself to be made a fool of or are turning a blind eye to someone's highly negative actions.

• *Wednesday 6 October* •

Fasten your seatbelt because it's going to be a bumpy day, thanks to the surprising and possibly even shocking antics of a certain someone. They may blow hot and cold so you don't know where you stand with them, or it could be a case of now you see them, now you don't. There's also a chance that you might be bowled over by someone you meet who isn't your usual type at all.

• *Thursday 7 October* •

There's a rather muted atmosphere between you and a loved one today, but it's probably nothing to worry about. Maybe they're busy with other things or it's just one of those days when you're both feeling preoccupied or reserved. One area in which you'll excel is creativity, especially if you're working on something that requires a steady hand and some dedicated concentration.

• *Friday 8 October* •

You'll have to pace yourself if you're supposed to be busy today, or you'll soon run out of energy and stamina. Yes, it's one of those days when you feel as though you're almost running on empty, with little in reserve. Be kind to yourself and keep away from anyone who's a germ factory, in case you succumb to whatever it is that ails them.

• *Saturday 9 October* •

You have a great eye for detail today, especially when tackling paperwork and official business matters. For instance, this would be an excellent day to fill in a complicated form or write a letter to the taxman. There's little danger of anyone being able to pull the wool over your eyes right now because you're really on the ball and you'll spot any half-truths in no time at all.

• *Sunday 10 October* •

This is a super day for making an effort to keep someone sweet, particularly if your relationship has been soured by recent events. You don't have to fawn all over them, but a little tact and consideration will work wonders now. It will also help not to mention your grievances but instead to talk about neutral topics that can't cause further bad feeling.

• *Monday 11 October* •

A certain someone is absolutely convinced that they know what's best for you, even if you don't agree with them. And they'll be very quick to make their pronouncements or lay down the law, even to the extent of contradicting you or taking matters into their own hands. This could be a pushy relative, partner or boss, but whoever it is, you strongly object to what they're doing.

• *Tuesday 12 October* •

If you're lucky you'll benefit from someone's generosity and benevolence today. Now, before you get all excited, I have to add that this doesn't necessarily mean that you'll be unwrapping a brand-new Mercedes in a colour that matches your eyes or wondering how to spend that large cheque you've just been given. The gift you receive will probably be much smaller and more modest, but it will be greatly appreciated by you nonetheless.

• *Wednesday 13 October* •

You need an extra layer of skin today in order to protect yourself from a loved one's harsh criticism and general carping. What's got into them, anyway? There could be an element of sour grapes in all this, perhaps because you've got something they want or they're jealous of your popularity. Try not to take it too seriously unless it's making life very unpleasant for you.

• *Thursday 14 October* •

Today's eclipsed New Moon will have a powerful impact on your joint and official finances over the next couple of weeks, giving you the chance to put them on a firmer or more balanced footing. An intimate relationship will also enter an exciting new phase, leading to some extremely satisfying developments between you.

• *Friday 15 October* •

This is a marvellous day for getting to the bottom of a mystery concerning a special person in your life. Perhaps you suspect that they're hiding something from you and you want to find out what it is, or you're desperate to discover whether their feelings for you are as strong as yours are for them. Well, you won't have to dig very deep to get the answers you're looking for!

• *Saturday 16 October* •

Life is looking pretty good today and you feel satisfied with your lot. Yes, things could be better but they could also be a great deal worse, and if you think about it you'll realize that you have plenty of reasons to count your blessings. These will be increased after you've spent time with someone who always makes your heart swell with love and pride.

• *Sunday 17 October* •

The more open-minded and tolerant you are today, the greater the amount of knowledge and information that you'll absorb. This is a fantastic day for learning something new, especially if it's outside your usual boundaries or requires a leap of the imagination. You're also remarkably brainy and clever right now, so make the most of this cerebral phase.

• *Monday 18 October* •

If something is bothering you, it will definitely help to confide in someone you trust. If you choose your confidant well, you may even find that you barely have to explain anything because they're so aware of what you're going through. Listen to what they say because it will contain some words of wisdom, even if you don't agree with absolutely everything you hear.

• *Tuesday 19 October* •

You're in a very gregarious and articulate frame of mind this Tuesday and will jump at the chance to get involved in discussions or wide-ranging conversations. If your social life isn't up to much at the moment, this is a good day for joining a club or organization that appeals to you and which might introduce you to lots of new friends. It's definitely worth a try!

• *Wednesday 20 October* •

Someone wants to make some serious changes to a situation but other people are blocking their progress. Whether you're the instigator of these changes or you feel as though you're the victim of them, you need to tread carefully today to avoid making things even worse than they are already. Watch out for a tendency to insist on calling the shots or to use emotional blackmail in order to get your own way.

• *Thursday 21 October* •

Quite frankly, your idea of heaven this Thursday is to retreat from the hustle and bustle of everyday life into a peaceful world of your own, and not to emerge until you feel better able to cope with other people again. If you can't do this physically, you'll do it emotionally or mentally and thereby give the impression of being elusive and possibly even rather ambiguous. Take care!

• *Friday 22 October* •

After yesterday's desire to enjoy as much peace and quiet as possible, you're now in the mood to throw yourself into the swing of things whenever you get the chance. It's a really good day for getting together with a special person in your life, whether you have romantic designs on them or you enjoy a different sort of relationship. It will feel great to be in their company.

• *Saturday 23 October* •

The next four weeks will find you on top form and really eager to get the most out of life. It's going to be a great time to take up challenges and get involved in activities that call for an adventurous and intrepid spirit. Anything that expands the horizons of your life will be right up your street now, and you never know where it will lead, either. So be daring!

• *Sunday 24 October* •

Your mind is working wonderfully well today. Your thoughts are ordered and logical, you're open-minded enough to be able to appreciate other people's points of view, and you're gripped by an insatiable curiosity about the world around you. You might simply read the papers from cover to cover, or decide to sign up for a class or course that you can really get your teeth into.

• *Monday 25 October* •

Relationships mean even more to you than usual today, with the emphasis on the atmosphere between you and a certain person. If things are going well with them, you'll have a spring in your step and feel on top of the world. But if things are going badly or are simply rather low-key at the moment, you'll feel wretched and will be ultra-sensitive to any indication that the situation is about to get worse.

• *Tuesday 26 October* •

You're in a much more emotionally resilient mood this Tuesday, making you better equipped to be able to see what's going on around you and to examine your relationships in the cold light of day. Rather than dwell on the negative aspects of your partnerships, it would be better to concentrate on the good points and to think about how you can accentuate these in the future so that they become a positive force between you.

• *Wednesday 27 October* •

This is a perfect day to introduce some changes that will benefit everyone concerned, particularly if these involve a joint financial matter, a bureaucratic problem or your job. However, it's very important to consult everyone before swinging into action, so that you've got their backing and they know what's going on. Honesty is your best policy right now.

• *Thursday 28 October* •

There's an eclipsed Full Moon today, and it will have a big effect on your communications over the next couple of weeks. Certain facts could come to light that need careful assessment, and which may even force you to re-evaluate some areas of your life. It's important to get at the truth now, even if you're wary of what it will lead to. There's no point in fooling yourself.

• *Friday 29 October* •

Between now and mid-November you'll get the chance to increase the sense of intimacy, affection and trust between you and a certain someone. This will be especially welcome if you've been together for ages and your relationship has long since lost its first fine careless rapture. Rekindle the spark that originally brought you together, so it continues to burn strongly.

• *Saturday 30 October* •

It's bad news if you want everything to run like clockwork today because that's unlikely to happen. Instead, chaos is likely to ensue when plans are changed at the eleventh hour, arrangements go wrong or you have to cope with a mini disaster. Take care when handling precious objects to avoid dropping or damaging them.

• *Sunday 31 October* •

Do you need to recover from yesterday's disruptive influences? Then set aside plenty of time for rest and relaxation this Sunday. Flop on the sofa with the papers, lose yourself in a favourite film or gather some of your nearest and dearest around you. You may also be assailed by waves of nostalgia at some point, possibly even making you rather tearful and sentimental.

NOVEMBER AT A GLANCE

Love	♥ ♥
Money	£ $ £ $
Career	💻 💻 💻 💻 💻
Health	☼ ☼

• *Monday 1 November* •

It's a very lively start to the month, with lots of enjoyable comings and goings. If you're out and about, you might bump into someone you weren't expecting to see but who's a sight for sore eyes. An unexpected invitation might also come your way, much to your delight. If you're out shopping, you'll enjoy buying items that are unusual or not your normal style.

• *Tuesday 2 November* •

A relationship will benefit enormously today if you're able to talk to this person from the heart. Forget about adopting your usual protective colouring or hedging your bets, and instead tell them exactly how you're feeling. Such honesty will be refreshing and will help to cement your relationship for the future.

• *Wednesday 3 November* •

This is another good day for working hard at a close relationship in order to improve it. You could be drawn into a conversation with each other in which you talk about matters that are dear to your hearts, or about things that you would normally keep to yourself. A child may need your guidance at some point, and you'll be most effective if you can give this with a light touch and plenty of humour.

• *Thursday 4 November* •

Throughout the rest of the year you'll benefit from thinking hard about your career, social status, long-term goals and your relationship with people you consider to be mentors. It will be a marvellous opportunity to talk seriously to the people you respect, as you'll be very interested in hearing what they have to say. They'll give you plenty of food for thought.

• *Friday 5 November* •

You're in the market for all the enjoyment and affection you can get today, and everything else will pale by comparison. You may even be tempted to cancel some arrangements or postpone some chores in order to have more free time. You're also feeling rather extravagant and are tempted to throw caution, and your cash, to the winds, whether or not you can afford it.

• *Saturday 6 November* •

You're extremely resistant to what someone is telling you this Saturday. Maybe you completely disagree with their opinions, think they're talking total nonsense, or are horrified by what they're saying. Be careful, because you could easily become locked in a stubborn battle of wills with this person, in which neither of you is prepared to yield a single inch.

• *Sunday 7 November* •

Yesterday's intransigence is a thing of the past and you're in a much more reasonable mood. So maybe you should mull over what happened and think hard about what you talked about. This is also an excellent day for being in touch with people who come from a different background, culture or religion, so you can learn more about one another's lives.

• *Monday 8 November* •

If you're a typical Piscean you can be pretty starry-eyed at the best of times, but you've really got it bad today! You're totally enamoured with a certain person and can't think about much else. It's wonderful to be floating on cloud nine like this, provided that the object of your affections is worthy of your admiration and love. If they aren't, you'll be in for a massive disappointment before too long.

• *Tuesday 9 November* •

The festive season may still seem a long way off but it isn't really and this is the perfect day to start thinking about it. You're in a very generous and warm-hearted mood, so you'll enjoy writing out a list of all the presents you've got to buy. You might even get so enthusiastic that you have to rush out to the shops and start buying some gifts while you're still in the mood.

• *Wednesday 10 November* •

This isn't the easiest of days, so take care. Maybe a loved one is being remote or unfriendly, or you feel completely flat when something that you were looking forward to is cancelled. Do your best to remain upbeat and positive, or every tiny snag will seem like a massive catastrophe and you'll end up feeling deeply sorry for yourself. Keep smiling, Pisces!

• *Thursday 11 November* •

You'll come up with some really clever ideas today, given half a chance. You're able to look at the bigger picture, especially if you're currently wrestling with a particular problem and have been in danger of not being able to see the wood for the trees. This is also a great opportunity to pick the brains of a financial or legal expert if needs be.

• *Friday 12 November* •

Your world is about to blossom and expand in all sorts of exciting directions, so try not to limit yourself in any way during the coming fortnight. You might get the chance to go travelling, learn something new or become involved in a challenging project. You stand to gain a tremendous amount from all these developments, especially if you approach them with optimism.

• *Saturday 13 November* •

Being born under the sensitive sign of Pisces means you have the knack of being able to tune in to the atmosphere around you, and today is no exception. In fact, you'll find it surprisingly easy to connect with others and to read between the lines. If you're in charge of a group of people you'll be able to adjust your behaviour to fit in with theirs and to get them on your side.

• *Sunday 14 November* •

You'll need all the patience you can muster if you're taking part in a family gathering because someone is being controlling and demanding. This might be an older relative who still treats you like a child, telling you what you should and shouldn't do. You won't have the heart to tell them to mind their own business, but they'll get on your nerves all the same.

• *Monday 15 November* •

You long to break out in some way today and to do things that you find emancipating and exciting, and which reflect your true personality. If anyone expects you to toe the party line or to do things you don't want to do, they'll be in for a rude awakening when you insist on going your own way instead. What happens now will be liberating and a huge blast of fresh air. It's great!

• *Tuesday 16 November* •

It would be a shame to spend too much time alone today, unless you're busy with intellectual topics that stretch your brain. You're in a highly gregarious mood and will absolutely revel in the company of kindred spirits, so it's a perfect day for getting together with friends. You'll also enjoy making exciting plans for your future.

• *Wednesday 17 November* •

Watch out because it's horribly easy today to open your mouth and put your foot in it. This will be even more likely if you're feeling agitated about something but are trying to hide it, as your pent-up irritation will find an outlet sooner or later. There could also be a discrepancy about what you think is funny and what someone else finds amusing, leading to some embarrassing moments.

• *Thursday 18 November* •

Ideally, you should lock yourself away from everyone else for a while today so you can get on with your work in peace. You have a strong need for solitude now, because that will be the best way to think things through. If you've been putting off some important business matters, such as writing official letters or completing forms, tackle them now while you're able to concentrate so well.

• *Friday 19 November* •

Just about every experience that you have today will add to your education in some way. For instance, you could learn a lot from having a conversation with a friend, or you might hear something very interesting on the radio or television. You're full of common sense right now, without seeming staid or stuffy, so you've got the best of both worlds.

• *Saturday 20 November* •

There's a constrained and tense atmosphere between you and a loved one, and it's starting to bother you. The burning question is whether you're tuning in to what's really happening or whether you're letting your fears get the better of you. Distract yourself by doing something that boosts your self-esteem and which doesn't rely on other people to make you feel good.

• *Sunday 21 November* •

You have the ability to penetrate deep below the surface of situations today to find out what's really going on. This will be very helpful if you're hoping to clear up a mystery or solve a problem, but beware of a tendency to become obsessed with finding answers to questions. This will make you appear very nosy and insensitive, prying into things that are nothing to do with you.

• *Monday 22 November* •

Between now and mid-December you'll absolutely love being able to spread your wings and explore the world. You'll jump at the prospect of doing some travelling, especially if this involves going abroad. You could also lose your heart to someone who comes from another country, or become smitten by a cause or campaign that you truly believe in. It's going to be a very interesting time!

• *Tuesday 23 November* •

Get to grips with your finances this Tuesday, especially if you're in danger of letting things slide. Go through your bank and credit card statements carefully, in case they contain mistakes or anomalies, and pay any overdue bills before you forget about them. You might also hear some interesting news about a pay rise or bonus that's coming your way.

• *Wednesday 24 November* •

Any hint of a restriction or limitation will make you want to scream today, because it's the last thing you need right now. In fact, you'll be tempted to rebel in dramatic and impressive ways if you think someone is trying to clip your wings or you're feeling hemmed in by repressive circumstances. Break free if needs be, but don't do it in ways that are designed to cause maximum disruption or to draw unnecessary attention to yourself.

• *Thursday 25 November* •

Go carefully today because it will be easy to lose track of what you're doing and get into a muddle. It doesn't help that you're feeling very absent-minded and forgetful, so you may also waste a lot of time searching for items that you've mislaid. Nevertheless, this is a marvellous day for letting rip with your imagination because it will take you on some fabulous journeys.

• *Friday 26 November* •

Over the coming fortnight you'll have to pay even more attention than usual to the needs and emotions of your nearest and dearest. If you don't, perhaps because you're busy with outside interests, you may end up having to sort out a mini crisis that someone has got themselves into. You may also find yourself saying goodbye to part of your past, which will be poignant.

• *Saturday 27 November* •

This is a wonderful day for concentrating on your creature comforts and for doing whatever will make your home feel more cosy and secure. It's almost inevitable that shopping will feature in your schedule, and you'll enjoy visiting some of your favourite shops to see what's on offer. If you're buying food, be aware that you could get carried away and bring home far too much.

• *Sunday 28 November* •

You'll leave no stone unturned in your quest to get at the truth of a situation this Sunday, even if it makes you extremely unpopular. But why are you doing this? Try to examine your motives very carefully, especially if you're starting to become obsessed about finding out what's going on. Your aggressive curiosity may even make others want to protect themselves.

• *Monday 29 November* •

It's important that you remain realistic about your prospects today; otherwise you'll soon get carried away and start to believe in your own wishful thinking. This is even more important if you're sorting out a big financial matter, because right now you'll talk yourself into believing almost anything if it will make you feel better.

• *Tuesday 30 November* •

Be very careful when dealing with bureaucratic matters over the next three weeks as they could easily go awry. Important letters could get lost in the post, e-mails may go astray or people might go back on their word. Ideally you should avoid signing on any dotted lines for the time being in case you're being hoodwinked in some way. Right now, it's better to be safe than sorry.

DECEMBER AT A GLANCE

Love	♥ ♥
Money	£ $ £
Career	💻 💻 💻 💻 💻
Health	☼ ☼ ☼

• *Wednesday 1 December* •

OK, it's the start of December and you need to get your skates on if you want to be ready for the forthcoming festivities. If you've barely made a dent in your preparations so far, sit down and start writing out your list of what needs to be done. Be as efficient as possible, because that's the best way to avert the sense of panic that's hovering in the air and waiting to strike.

• *Thursday 2 December* •

You'll get a tremendous amount of work done today if you organize your time well. This will apply whether you're working on your own or as part of a team, because either way you'll know exactly what you're doing and will take pride in doing it to the best of your ability. If you're taking part in a meeting or attending an interview, you'll show yourself in a really favourable light.

• *Friday 3 December* •

Go carefully because you're in rather a gullible mood today, making you very vulnerable to people who might want to mislead you in some way. Unfortunately, you'll also do a very good job of misleading yourself by deliberately turning a blind eye to difficult situations and taking an escapist attitude to anything that seems like too much hard work. Don't persist in this for too long: it will inevitably lead to trouble.

• *Saturday 4 December* •

You're still keen to keep well clear of anything or anyone that looks like being a problem, but at least you aren't being as escapist as you were yesterday. This is a marvellous day for taking care of someone who isn't very well at the moment or who needs all the sympathy and understanding you can give them.

• *Sunday 5 December* •

A powerful sense of adventure sweeps over you today, making you eager to rise to challenges and to pick up the gauntlet that life throws at your feet. There will be a certain amount of daring and courage in all this, and you might even surprise yourself by getting involved in situations that would normally send you running in the opposite direction.

• *Monday 6 December* •

You're capable of making some very constructive and important decisions today, particularly where your relations with certain people are concerned. If you're fed up with the way someone has been treating you, you might now decide that the worm is about to turn and you're going to be much firmer about what you're prepared to put up with and what you won't tolerate.

• *Tuesday 7 December* •

You have a one-track mind this Tuesday and it's running along very ambitious lines! You might be absolutely determined to achieve something that you've been attempting for ages, and be so committed to it that you're prepared to let everything else go by the wayside for the time being. That's great, but don't become obsessive about it.

• *Wednesday 8 December* •

You could have a lucky break today when fate steps in and takes a hand. For instance, a situation may seem to be heading for disaster when you're suddenly bailed out in ways you would never have imagined. However, this doesn't mean you can take foolish risks in the hope that things will work out OK because there's no guaranteeing that they'll do so automatically.

• *Thursday 9 December* •

The last thing you want to do today is to take your time over anything. Instead, you've got one eye permanently on the clock and you're trying to cram as many activities into the day as possible. This will be good fun and you'll enjoy keeping up the momentum, but beware of a possible tendency to become reckless or to try to cut corners in order to save time, as this will be self-defeating in the long run.

• *Friday 10 December* •

Ask someone for their advice and they'll still be talking half an hour later. Unfortunately, even though they're saying a lot, there may not be many pearls of wisdom in their conversation and you may quickly decide that they're just yakking on about whatever has popped into their head, with little or no relevance to what you asked them in the first place. Ho hum!

• *Saturday 11 December* •

You'll value the chance to have some time to yourself today, even if you have to snatch the odd moment here and there. It's important for you to recharge your mental and physical batteries at every opportunity, or you'll soon feel tired and frazzled. This is an ideal day to practise some form of meditation or creative visualization because it will go really well.

• *Sunday 12 December* •

Have you started to think about your New Year resolutions? If not, give them plenty of attention over the coming fortnight because then they'll be able to benefit from the energy of today's New Moon. Don't be afraid to set yourself some high targets – you stand an excellent chance of reaching them. This is no time to underestimate your abilities, Pisces!

• *Monday 13 December* •

Someone is in a no-nonsense mood. This makes them rather formidable company because they aren't mucking about and they don't want to waste their time. Instead, they're very single-minded about getting what they want and they won't care who gets trampled on in the process. Be careful if this person sees you as a stepping stone towards getting what they want, as they could be quite ruthless in the way they treat you.

• *Tuesday 14 December* •

This is a super day for understanding what's going on under the surface of things and for tuning in to the subtle messages that others are sending out. For instance, someone may say one thing yet you'll be utterly convinced that they really mean something quite different. However, they won't like it if you say so, so you'll have to maintain a tactful and discreet silence.

• *Wednesday 15 December* •

If you want to make the best of the day you should lock yourself away and work on your own. This will make it easier to concentrate, especially if you're trying to focus on something that's fiddly or difficult. If you've got something on your mind at the moment it will be worth having a quiet word in someone's ear; this person will help you to get things into their proper perspective.

• *Thursday 16 December* •

From today, you'll be in a better position to get on well with someone who has power or authority over you. This might be your boss, some other authority figure, a friend you really respect or an older relative. So maybe you should chat up your superiors at the office Christmas party, or make more of an effort to understand what makes a certain person tick.

• *Friday 17 December* •

Are you feeling fraught? It certainly seems that way, perhaps because you've got far too much on your plate and not nearly enough time to tackle it all. Do yourself a big favour and start with whatever is most urgent; otherwise you'll waste time by dithering or getting caught up in trivial tasks. Above all, don't get into a panic, because that will squander valuable time and energy.

• *Saturday 18 December* •

If you-know-who has been getting on your nerves recently, matters will soon come to a head and force you to take drastic action. You might finally lose your rag with someone who's been testing your patience to the limit, or have to stand your ground if you feel you're being messed about in some way. Clear the air if needs be but don't create a really nasty atmosphere by throwing an eye-popping tantrum.

• *Sunday 19 December* •

You're usually pretty easy-going but your levels of tolerance have dropped dramatically today, leaving you chafing at the merest suggestion of restrictions or emotional pressure. It will be far better to let off steam before you feel as though you're about to blow your top, because that will prevent you doing or saying things that will really put the cat among the pigeons.

• *Monday 20 December* •

Communications with officialdom haven't always been easy this December but fortunately they get back on track from today. This gives you just enough time to sort out any lingering problems before the Christmas holidays begin in earnest. If you're being pushed to sign a document or agreement, make sure you read the small print carefully first. You don't want to be caught out!

• *Tuesday 21 December* •

Your friendships come under the spotlight from today and they'll continue to light up your life for the next four weeks. This will be a marvellous opportunity to get together with chums who you haven't seen lately, so how about arranging a big party if you haven't got anything planned? This will also be your cue to focus on your hopes and wishes for the future.

• *Wednesday 22 December* •

You're lacking in energy and resources today, which will soon slow you down and make you feel as though you're wading through treacle. The only way to cope is to have as many breaks as possible, and not to set yourself impossible goals that you could never hope to meet. You're also very susceptible to the criticisms or put-downs of others, but do your best to ignore them.

• *Thursday 23 December* •

Someone is in a very boisterous mood today and you may want to make yourself scarce after a short spell in their company. Their idea of a joke may be your idea of extreme rudeness, or they could take pleasure in being argumentative just for the sake of it. Don't let this person wind you up; if they do, you'll end up going off pop through sheer tension!

• *Friday 24 December* •

Although you're busy putting the finishing touches to your Christmas preparations, you'll also have to pay attention to someone who's feeling neglected or unloved. Luckily it won't take much to make this person feel better, so a big hug or a little consideration might do the trick. You should also bear in mind that they may be feeling nostalgic or sad about the past.

• *Saturday 25 December* •

There's little doubt about who's the life and soul of the party today, because it's you! You're in a really good mood and you're keen to make sure that everyone has a wonderful day. It looks as though things won't go entirely according to plan, but you'll manage to take all the unexpected developments in your stride and even to turn them to your advantage. Happy Christmas!

• *Sunday 26 December* •

Today's Full Moon will raise questions in your mind about a loved one over the next two weeks. You might wonder what they're playing at and have to ask them to be straight with you, or you could work hard at overcoming the current problems between you so you're able to enter a much more positive phase in your relationship.

• *Monday 27 December* •

You're blessed with huge dollops of discretion and diplomacy today, which will come in very handy when you have to choose your words carefully with a certain person. At some point you could find yourself on the receiving end of someone's deepest, darkest secrets, in which case you'll have to treat these with respect and promise to keep them to yourself.

• *Tuesday 28 December* •

This is another brilliant day for being tactful, and if anything you'll be even more successful than you were yesterday. This is not to be sneezed at, so seize the opportunity to talk to people who can sometimes be very touchy or who need to be handled with kid gloves. If you meet someone who's older or more influential than you, you'll be a big hit with them.

• *Wednesday 29 December* •

Whether the excesses of the past few days are catching up with you or you're feeling drained for other reasons, you need as much rest as possible today. Once you get tired, your defences will be down and you'll start to fret about whatever is currently nagging away at the back of your mind. You're also concerned about the welfare of a certain person, which doesn't help.

• *Thursday 30 December* •

You're thinking along very inventive lines today, which is brilliant if you're trying to decide what you want to achieve in 2005. Get out a notebook or diary and start jotting down your ideas, so there's no danger of forgetting them. Discussing some of your plans with someone you respect could lead to even more brainwaves, and will assure you of their moral and emotional support.

• *Friday 31 December* •

Someone is extremely headstrong and defiant today, and there's every chance that you're the one fitting this description. If so, what's got into you? The more others are trying to make you behave yourself or do what they want, the more determined you'll be to do the exact opposite. Show them that you're an individual in your own right without going completely overboard about it, because that will cause trouble. Then, once you've got all that off your chest, you can relax and look forward to a really Happy New Year!

YOUR PISCES SUN SIGN

In this chapter I am going to tell you all about your Pisces Sun sign. But what is a Sun sign? It often gets called a star sign, but are they the same thing? Well, yes, although 'Sun sign' is a more accurate term. Your Sun sign is the sign that the Sun occupied when you were born. Every year, the Sun moves through the heavens and spends an average of 30 days in each of the twelve signs. When you were born, the Sun was moving through the sign of Pisces, so this is your Sun or star sign.

This chapter tells you everything you want to know about your Pisces Sun sign. To start off, I describe your general personality – what makes you tick. Then I talk about your attitude to relationships, the way you handle money, what your Sun sign says about your health and, finally, which careers are best for you. Put all that together and you will have a well-rounded picture of yourself.

Character

Yours is the last sign of the zodiac, and one astrological theory maintains that Pisces contains a little of each of the other eleven signs. Some people even believe that being born with the Sun in Pisces means you won't have to be reincarnated again on earth!

However, it doesn't seem quite that simple. Pisces is the sign of the saint and the sinner. There are some Pisceans who have so much compassion that they don't seem human at all, while other members of this sign don't seem human for very different and sinister reasons. You're ruled by Neptune, the planet of dreams, imagination and confusion. Neptune can give you tremendous sympathy for other people but it can also make you unsure of what you're doing. Many Pisceans say that they drift through life, not knowing what they are meant to be doing and without any distinct goals. They allow themselves to be led by other people and by circumstances, rather than make autonomous decisions. Neptune can also cloud your judgement, in extreme cases even to the point where you're unable to stop yourself doing something wrong.

Neptune also makes you very idealistic. When coupled with your Water element, this means you're extremely sensitive and can easily be hurt by others. You're also sensitive in other ways because you quickly absorb the atmosphere around you, whether it's positive or negative. It may help to take protective measures if you have to be with people who really disturb you.

Many Pisceans have psychic powers or highly developed extrasensory perception. You may experience this through hunches and gut feelings, or you might have prophetic dreams. As with any other gift, the more you use it, the better developed it will become.

Relationships

It's very important for you to be choosy about who you spend your time with because you're so easily influenced by other people. You can feel quite ill if you have to spend too long with people you don't like or whose attitude to life is in sharp contrast to yours. This is because you can absorb part of their energy and it may not do you much good!

However, you always like to think the best of people until proved wrong. Even then, you'll give them the benefit of the doubt for as long as possible. You believe that finding fault with others somehow diminishes you in the process. You are also very aware that you may not behave perfectly all the time yourself, so you feel you have little right to criticize others.

Your idealism can lead to broken hearts and hurt feelings because it means that you tend to put people on pedestals and you keep them there until they prove they've got feet of clay. You are then profoundly disappointed and may even lose faith in other people if you feel you were completely betrayed.

You enjoy having a partner around and you'll do whatever you can to make them happy and contented. Sometimes this means putting your own needs second. You don't mind doing this but in the end it may lead to resentment in you and an ingrained selfishness in the other person. You're also a confirmed romantic and you need a partner who understands this and will make a huge fuss of you!

Money

This is rather a sore point for most Pisceans! Pisces isn't a sign that's associated with vast amounts of money. For a start, when you've got it you often prefer to give it away rather than keep it all. You're very kind and generous, and you also can't bear to see people in trouble so you like to help in any way you can, even if all you do is drop a couple of coins in a collecting tin. It's also true that many Pisceans struggle to manage their money effectively. If this sounds like you, it may be because you hate dealing with unpleasant facts, so you prefer to ignore the subject of your bank balance or your overloaded credit card altogether.

Also, it's a rare Piscean who values money for its own sake. You can't see the point in being like Scrooge and hoarding your cash. You find something distasteful in the very idea, especially when you need only to switch on the TV news to hear about people who are struggling to survive.

However, this doesn't mean that you don't like shopping and spending money! You enjoy looking good and you have a weakness for beautiful objects. You also like buying things on the spur of the moment. Exotic holidays are another way of indulging yourself, when you can afford them.

Health

Being such a sensitive sign, you need to look after yourself. You don't always have as much stamina as you'd like and you certainly need to make sure you get plenty of rest. You also appreciate having time to yourself because it enables you to recuperate and recharge your batteries. If you have a busy life or live with others, it's even more important for you to be alone at some point every day, even if it's only when you're in the bathroom. Ideally, though, you should set aside a few minutes every day when you're left completely undisturbed.

It can be hard for you to unwind at times, so a relaxation technique will be very valuable. You might like to try yoga, meditation or creative visualization. You might also benefit from working with crystals or essential oils. Being in or near water can also help you to feel better.

With such a delicate metabolism, it's important that you choose your food and drink carefully. You might be allergic to certain foods or find that too much alcohol makes you feel lousy. Organic food, if you can afford it, may make quite a difference to your general health and you may also benefit from a vegetarian or semi-vegetarian diet.

Pisces rules the feet, so it's no surprise that the vast majority of Pisceans have problems finding comfortable shoes. It may help to visit a good chiropodist or podiatrist. If you're interested in complementary therapies, you may find that you respond especially well to reflexology because it's practised on the feet.

Career

Forget about getting involved in any dog-eat-dog profession. You're unlikely to enjoy it because it simply isn't in your nature to be ruthlessly ambitious. You'll feel like a fish out of water, which is bad news, as you belong to the sign of the fish!

Ideally, you need a career that enables you to express your tremendous compassion and ability to care for other people. Anything that puts you in touch with the public is good, and it's even better if you're working in the medical profession or in an institution. You can also be drawn to a career connected with religion or spirituality. Charity or voluntary work can appeal. Whatever you do for a living, it's important that you work with people you like. You will also prefer a job that enables you to express your creativity.

Pisces is a sign of contrasts, of highs and lows. Many Pisceans are magnetically attracted to glamorous careers, while many others are drawn towards jobs that are anything but! So the film industry and beauty business are both full of Pisceans, and so is the prison service!

LOVE AND THE STARS

Have you ever noticed that you get on better with some signs than others? Perhaps all your friends belong to only a few signs or you've never hit it off with people who come from a particular sign. Or maybe you've recently met someone from a sign that you aren't familiar with at all, and you're wondering how your relationship will develop. Well, this chapter gives you a brief insight into your relationship with the other Sun signs. Check the combination under your own sign's heading first, then read about your relationship from the viewpoint of the other sign to find out what they think of you. It could be very revealing!

At the end of this chapter you'll find two compatibility charts that tell you, at a glance, how well you get on with the other signs as lovers and as friends. Look for the woman's Sun sign along the top of the chart and then find the man's sign down the side. The box where the two meet will show how well they get on together.

Even if your current relationship gets a low score from the charts, that doesn't mean it won't last. It simply indicates that you'll have to work harder at this relationship than at others.

Pisces

Pisces and **Pisces** is wonderful if you're both prepared to face facts rather than pretend your relationship is something it's not. Your life is likely to be highly romantic and you'll love creating a sophisticated home together.

Pisces and **Aries** will be very trying at times. It may also be painful, since your Arien is unlikely to understand how easily you're hurt. Even so, they will encourage you to grow another layer of skin and to laugh at yourself.

Pisces and **Taurus** is a very sensual combination. You'll bring out the romantic in one another, but there will be times when you'll wish your Taurean were less matter-of-fact, practical and sensible.

Pisces and **Gemini** can have fun together but it's awfully easy for you to feel hurt by your Gemini's glib turns of phrase. You may be happier as friends than lovers because your emotional needs are so different.

Pisces and **Cancer** is super because you both express love in the same way. It's wonderful being with someone who takes such care of you, although your Cancerian may not understand your need to be left alone sometimes.

Pisces and **Leo** find it hard to understand each other. At times you may find your Leo rather grand. You share a pronounced artistic streak and you're both very affectionate, but is that enough to keep you together?

Pisces and **Virgo** can be difficult for you. Your Virgo may trample all over your feelings in their well-meaning efforts to point out your faults and help you to rise above them. It all sounds like a lot of unnecessary criticism to you.

Pisces and **Libra** can be incredibly romantic. You could easily have a heady affair straight out of a Hollywood weepie, but staying together is another matter. You may drift apart because you're reluctant to face up to problems.

Pisces and **Scorpio** is a highly emotional and complex pairing. You're both very deep and sensitive, and it may take a while before you begin to understand each other. Once that happens, you won't look back.

Pisces and **Sagittarius** is dicey because you won't know what to make of your forthright Sagittarian. Why are they so blunt? Can't they see that it upsets you? You may be better as friends who share lots of exploits.

Pisces and **Capricorn** is fine if your Capricorn is happy to show their feelings. But if they're buttoned up or repressed, you won't know how to get through to them. Even so, you'll love the way they provide for you.

Pisces and **Aquarius** may as well be talking different languages for all the sense you make to each other. They enjoy talking about ideas that leave you baffled but will struggle to express their emotions in the way you need.

Aries

Aries and **Aries** is a very energetic combination, and you encourage each other in many different ways. Your relationship is competitive, sexy, exciting and sometimes pretty tempestuous!

Aries and **Taurus** can be difficult because you don't always understand each other. You love your Taurean's loyalty and affection but can feel frustrated if they're a great traditionalist or very stubborn.

Aries and **Gemini** get on like a house on fire and love hatching up new schemes together. But your differing sexual needs could cause problems, especially if your Gemini doesn't share your high sex drive.

Aries and **Cancer** is fine if your Cancerian will give you lots of personal freedom. However, they may be hurt if you aren't at home as much as they'd like, and they'll wonder what you're up to while you're away.

Aries and **Leo** really hit it off well and you'll have a lot of fun together. Sometimes you may wish your Leo would unbend a bit and be less dignified, but you adore the way they love and cherish you. It's great for your ego!

Aries and **Virgo** can be tricky because you have so little in common. You like to rush through life taking each day as it comes while they prefer to plan things in advance and then worry if they're doing the right thing. Irritating!

Aries and **Libra** have a lot to learn from each other. You enjoy the odd skirmish while your Libran prefers to keep the peace. Try to compromise over your differences rather than make them either/or situations.

Aries and **Scorpio** can be very dynamic and sexy together. Power is a huge aphrodisiac for you both so you're greatly attracted to each other. If you're a flirtatious Aries, your Scorpio will soon clip your wings.

Aries and **Sagittarius** are really excited by each other's company. You both adore challenges and will spur one another on to further feats and adventures. Your sex life is lively and interesting, and will keep you pretty busy.

Aries and **Capricorn** may not seem to have much in common on the surface. Yet you are both ambitious and will enjoy watching each other's progress. Sexually, things are surprisingly highly charged and naughty.

Aries and **Aquarius** have a lot of fun together but also share plenty of sparring matches. You get on better as friends than lovers because your Aquarian may not be nearly as interested in sex as you are.

Aries and **Pisces** is one of those tricky combinations that needs a lot of care if it's to succeed. It's horribly easy for you to upset your Piscean, often without realizing it, and you may get bored with having to reassure them so much.

Taurus

Taurus and **Taurus** is great because you're with someone who understands you inside out. Yet although this is comforting at first, it might start to become rather boring after a while, especially if you both like playing it safe.

Taurus and **Gemini** is good for keeping you on your toes, although you may find this tiring in the long term. They need a lot of change and variety, which can unsettle you and make you cling to stability and tradition.

Taurus and **Cancer** is lovely. You both appreciate the same sorts of things in life, such as good food, a loving partner and a cosy home. Once you get together you'll feel as though you've found your true soulmate.

Taurus and **Leo** share a love of luxury and the good things in life. You also know you can trust your Leo to be faithful and loyal, and in return you will shower them with plenty of admiration and moral support.

Taurus and **Virgo** is a very practical combination. Neither of you likes wasting time or money, although you may sometimes wish that your Virgo could be a little less austere and a bit more relaxed. But you still love them.

Taurus and **Libra** can have a very sensual and loving relationship. Neither of you likes conflict and you both need affectionate partners. But you may end up spending a lot of money together on all sorts of luxuries.

Taurus and **Scorpio** is a very powerful combination, especially in the bedroom. You both place a lot of importance on fidelity and loyalty, and you'll both believe that your relationship is the most important thing in your lives.

Taurus and **Sagittarius** don't really understand each other. You enjoy your home comforts and are generally content with life, while your Sagittarian always finds the grass is greener on the other side of the fence.

Taurus and **Capricorn** have a lot in common. You're both lusty, earthy and full of common sense. If you aren't careful, your relationship could get bogged down in practicalities, making you neglect the fun side of things.

Taurus and **Aquarius** struggle to appreciate each other. You enjoy sticking to the status quo whenever possible, while your Aquarian is always thinking of the future. You're both very stubborn, so rows can end in stalemate.

Taurus and **Pisces** is fine if your Piscean has their feet on the ground, because then you'll enjoy their sensitivity. But if they're very vague or other-worldly, you'll soon get annoyed and lose patience with them.

Taurus and **Aries** isn't the easiest combination for you. Although you enjoy your Arien's enthusiasm, it can wear a bit thin sometimes, especially when they're keen on something that you think is unrealistic or too costly.

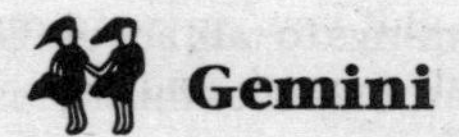

Gemini

Gemini and **Gemini** can be great fun or one big headache. You both crave variety and busy lives, but if you're both very sociable you may rarely see each other. Your sex life may also fizzle out over time.

Gemini and **Cancer** is tricky if you're lovers rather than friends. Although you'll adore your Cancerian's displays of affection at first, after a while they may seem rather clingy or will make you feel trapped.

Gemini and **Leo** have lots of fun together. You genuinely like and love one another, although you may secretly be amused sometimes by your Leo's regal behaviour and want to give them some gentle teasing.

Gemini and **Virgo** hit it off surprisingly well. There's so much for you to talk about and plenty of scope for having a good laugh. You're tremendous friends, whether your relationship is sexual or purely platonic.

Gemini and **Libra** is one of the most enjoyable combinations of all for you. You can encourage your easy-going Libran to be more assertive while they help you to relax, and also bring out the romance in your soul.

Gemini and **Scorpio** make uncomfortable bedfellows but good friends. You have very little in common sexually but are intrigued by each other's minds. You share an insatiable curiosity about human nature.

Gemini and **Sagittarius** have a really good time together. You especially enjoy learning new things from one another and never run out of things to talk about. Travel and books are just two of your many shared enthusiasms.

Gemini and **Capricorn** isn't very easy because you're so different. At first you're intrigued by your Capricorn's responsibility and common sense, but after a while they may seem a little staid or stuffy for you.

Gemini and **Aquarius** are fantastic friends. You're used to having the upper hand intellectually with people but here is someone who makes you think and encourages you to look at life in a new way.

Gemini and **Pisces** can be tricky because it's easy to hurt your Piscean's feelings without even realizing it. Neither of you is very keen on facing up to harsh reality, which causes problems if you both avoid dealing with the facts.

Gemini and **Aries** is tremendous fun and you'll spend a lot of time laughing. If even half the plans you make come to fruition, you'll have a fantastic time together with never a dull moment.

Gemini and **Taurus** can make you wonder what you're doing wrong. Your Taurean may seem bemused or even slightly alarmed by you, and positively threatened by your need for as much variety in your life as possible.

Cancer

Cancer and **Cancer** is wonderful because you're able to take refuge in each other. You'll lavish a lot of time and effort on your home. Problems will arise if one of you doesn't get on well with the other one's family or friends.

Cancer and **Leo** share a love of family life, and you may even agree to give it priority over everything else. You'll be very proud of your Leo's achievements but will fret if these take them away from home too often.

Cancer and **Virgo** have a lot to teach each other. You'll learn from your Virgo how to do things methodically and carefully, and you'll encourage them to be more demonstrative and loving. It should work well!

Cancer and **Libra** is great if you have shared goals. You both understand the importance of ambition and will readily support one another. You enjoy being with someone who isn't afraid to show their affection.

Cancer and **Scorpio** is a very emotional and satisfying pairing. You know you can reveal your true feelings to your Scorpio, and you'll encourage them to do the same with you. Sexually, you'll really be in your element.

Cancer and **Sagittarius** find it hard to appreciate each other. You may even feel as though you come from different planets because you operate on a very emotional level while your Sagittarian prefers to stick to the facts.

Cancer and **Capricorn** is a case of opposites attracting. You both need what the other one can offer, and you'll be especially pleased if your Capricorn's capacity for hard work will provide a roof over your head and a stable home.

Cancer and **Aquarius** can be quirky friends but you'll struggle to sustain an emotional relationship because you're chalk and cheese. Your need for love and reassurance may be very difficult for your Aquarian to deal with.

Cancer and **Pisces** are really happy together. It's great knowing that you're with someone who understands your deep emotional needs and your complicated personality. You'll also revel in taking care of your Piscean.

Cancer and **Aries** can work if you both make allowances for each other. You need to give your Aries a lot of freedom because they'll get very angry if they feel they're tied to your apron strings.

Cancer and **Taurus** is a marriage made in heaven. You both need a happy, comfortable home and you also share a love of food. Your relationship may be so self-sufficient that you barely need anyone else in your lives.

Cancer and **Gemini** is OK if you don't spend too much time together! You'll feel slightly threatened by your Gemini's need for an active and independent social life, and they'll resent being expected to spend so much time at home.

Leo

Leo and **Leo** is a very strong combination but there could be a few battles for power every now and then. After all, neither of you likes to relinquish the reins and hand over control to anyone else. Even so, you'll have a lot of fun.

Leo and **Virgo** is fine if you're prepared for some give and take but it won't be very easy if each of you stands your ground. You'll be pleased if your Virgo tries to help or advise you, but will be hurt if this turns to undue criticism.

Leo and **Libra** is a delicious pairing because it brings together the two signs of love. You'll adore being with someone who is so considerate, although their lack of decisiveness may sometimes make you grit your teeth with irritation.

Leo and **Scorpio** is wonderful until you have a row. At that point, you'll both refuse to budge an inch and admit that you might be in the wrong. You both set a lot of store by status symbols, which could work out expensive.

Leo and **Sagittarius** is great for keeping each other amused. You're both enthusiastic, intuitive and expansive, although you could sometimes be annoyed if your Sagittarian's social life prevents you seeing much of them.

Leo and **Capricorn** share a tremendous love of family and you'll enjoy creating a happy home together. Don't expect your Capricorn to be instinctively demonstrative: you may have to teach them to be more open.

Leo and **Aquarius** understand each other even if you don't always see eye to eye. Sometimes you can be left speechless by your plain-speaking Aquarian, and disappointed by their occasional reluctance to be cuddly.

Leo and **Pisces** bring out each other's creativity. This is a superb artistic partnership but may not be such good news if you're trying to maintain a sexual relationship because you have so little in common.

Leo and **Aries** have terrific fun together and will share many adventures. You'll enjoy making lots of plans, even if they don't always work out. You'll also spend plenty of money on lavishly entertaining your friends.

Leo and **Taurus** is the sort of relationship that makes you feel you know where you stand. You love knowing that your Taurean is steadfast and true, and that together you make a formidable team.

Leo and **Gemini** is a fun-filled combination that you really enjoy. You're stunned by your Gemini's endless inventiveness and their versatility, although you may secretly believe that they spread themselves too thin.

Leo and **Cancer** is great if you both need a comfortable and cosy home. But you may soon feel hemmed in if your Cancerian wants to restrict your social circle to nothing but family and close friends. You need more scope than that.

Virgo

Virgo and **Virgo** can endure many storms together, even though it's tough going at times. Here is someone who completely understands your interesting mixture of quirky individualism and the need to conform.

Virgo and **Libra** get on well together up to a point but can then come unstuck. It annoys you when your Libran fails to stand up for themselves and you don't understand why they're so touchy when you point out their faults.

Virgo and **Scorpio** are both fascinated by the details of life and you'll spend many happy hours analysing people's characters. Try not to be too brusque when pointing out some of your Scorpio's stranger points; they won't like it!

Virgo and **Sagittarius** is a very sociable pairing and you'll enjoy being together. You'll also have some fascinating conversations in which you both learn a lot. Sexually, it will either be great or ghastly.

Virgo and **Capricorn** really understand each other. You appreciate your Capricorn's reliability but worry about their workaholic tendencies. You'll both benefit from being openly affectionate and loving with one another.

Virgo and **Aquarius** enjoy discussing just about everything under the sun. But you'll quickly get irritated by your Aquarian's idiosyncratic views and their insistence that they're always right. Surely if anyone's right, you are?

Virgo and **Pisces** is not the easiest combination you can choose. If your Piscean finds it hard to face up to reality, you won't be sympathetic because you simply can't understand such an ostrich-like attitude.

Virgo and **Aries** struggle to get on well as close partners. You simply don't understand each other. They make a mess and you like things to be tidy. They rush into things and you like to take your time. There is little common ground.

Virgo and **Taurus** love each other's company. You both like to keep your feet on the ground and you share a healthy respect for money. You also have a very raunchy time in the bedroom although you don't advertise that fact.

Virgo and **Gemini** is a super combination for friendship or business. You think along similar lines and both excel at being flexible. However, in a sexual relationship you may fail to appreciate each other's finer points.

Virgo and **Cancer** is a great team. You like to take care of worldly matters while your Cancerian creates a happy and cosy home. If they collect a lot of clutter you'll think of it as dust traps rather than delightful keepsakes.

Virgo and **Leo** find it hard to understand each other because you're so different. You may secretly find your Leo rather ostentatious and there could be rows about the amount of money they spend. Try to live and let live.

Libra

Libra and **Libra** get on really well provided at least one of you is decisive and able to say what they think sometimes.

You'll appreciate one another's consideration, sensitivity and intelligence. A great combination!

Libra and **Scorpio** are good friends but may not understand each other's sexual and emotional needs. You may feel uncomfortable with the brooding, intense moods of your Scorpio, wishing they took things less seriously.

Libra and **Sagittarius** have lots of fun together, especially when it comes to discussing ideas and taking off on jaunts. However, you could be rather nonplussed, and possibly even hurt, by your Sagittarian's blunt comments.

Libra and **Capricorn** get on famously if you share goals. You understand each other's need to work hard towards your ambitions. But you'll have to coax your Capricorn into being as demonstrative and loving as you'd like.

Libra and **Aquarius** appreciate one another's minds. You may be better friends than lovers, because you could be bemused and hurt if your Aquarian is unnerved by your need for romance and idealism.

Libra and **Pisces** share a need for peace and harmony. You'll adore being with someone who's so artistic and sensitive, but you both need to balance your romantic natures with hefty doses of reality every now and then.

Libra and **Aries** are a great example of how opposites can attract. You admire the way your brave Arien can be so outspoken, and they may even manage to teach you to stand up for yourself.

Libra and **Taurus** share a love of beauty and an appreciation of the finer things in life. At first you may think you've found your perfect partner, although you may get irritated if your Taurean is very placid.

Libra and **Gemini** get on well in every sort of relationship. You're amused by your Gemini's butterfly ability to flit from one topic to the next and will enjoy encouraging them to discover the romance that lurks inside them.

Libra and **Cancer** enjoy one another's company. You love the way your Cancerian so obviously cares about your welfare and happiness, and it does you good to be the one who's fussed over for a change.

Libra and **Leo** can be a very expensive combination! Neither of you is frightened to spend money and together you can have a field day. Emotionally, you revel in one another's company because you're both born romantics.

Libra and **Virgo** have to make a lot of effort to appreciate one another. You can understand the importance of attending to details but you may secretly think that your Virgo sometimes is too much of a nit-picker.

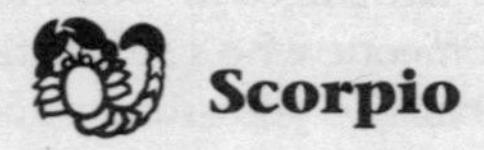

Scorpio

Scorpio and **Scorpio** feel safe with each other. You both know what you're capable of, good and bad. It's great to be with someone who matches you for intensity, but you might wind each other up and feed each other's neuroses.

Scorpio and **Sagittarius** can miss each other by miles. Even as friends, it's hard to understand one another. You like to zero in on the details while your Sagittarian prefers to take a broad view of the entire situation.

Scorpio and **Capricorn** bring out the best in one another, but it can take a little time. You enjoy the serious side to your Capricorn but you can also have some great laughs together. You also love knowing that they're so reliable.

Scorpio and **Aquarius** can have some terrific rows! You both have a tendency to be dogmatic and it's even worse when you get together. You can feel threatened if your Aquarian isn't as openly affectionate as you'd like.

Scorpio and **Pisces** share some powerful moments together. You love the complexity and sensitivity of your Piscean but will soon become suspicious if you think they're holding out on you or are playing games behind your back.

Scorpio and **Aries** is a tempestuous combination. Your temper builds up from a slow burn while your Arien will have a quick tantrum and then forget about it. Sexually, you'll have more than met your match.

Scorpio and **Taurus** complement each other in many ways. You're both loyal and loving, and you both need a secure home. However, problems will arise if one or both of you is possessive and jealous.

Scorpio and **Gemini** hit it off as friends but will struggle to stick together as lovers. You like to explore the nitty-gritty of situations while your Gemini apparently prefers to skim the surface. You may wonder if you can trust them.

Scorpio and **Cancer** can enjoy a highly emotional and satisfying relationship. You understand one another's needs and will take great delight in creating a stable and happy home life together.

Scorpio and **Leo** is tricky if you both want to rule the roost. Neither of you likes to relinquish control of situations, which can lead to some stormy battles for power. At times you may be jealous of your Leo's huge circle of friends.

Scorpio and **Virgo** have some wonderfully analytical conversations. You both enjoy digging below the surface to find out what's really going on. If it's a sexual relationship, its success will rest on what happens in the bedroom.

Scorpio and **Libra** appreciate one another but you may sometimes wish your Libran could be more forceful and dynamic. It will drive you mad when they sit on the fence or bend over backwards to please everyone.

Sagittarius and **Sagittarius** will either have a whale of a time or never see each other. If you both have wide-ranging interests, it may be difficult to make enough time for one another and you may eventually drift apart.

Sagittarius and **Capricorn** think of each other as a creature from another planet. You like your Capricorn's common sense but will soon get fed up if they cling to tradition, are a workaholic or never want to take any risks.

Sagittarius and **Aquarius** have a fantastic time together. You share so many interests that there is always something to talk about, with some far-ranging discussions. But you may wish your Aquarian were less pedantic.

Sagittarius and **Pisces** enjoy being friends but it can be difficult to understand each other as lovers. You like your Piscean's sensitivity but wish they weren't quite so easily hurt when you make off-the-cuff comments.

Sagittarius and **Aries** is great fun. You'll have all sorts of adventures together, with exotic holidays a particular indulgence. You're both pretty outspoken and your no-holds-barred rows will raise the roof.

Sagittarius and **Taurus** struggle to hit it off. You're so different that it's hard to find much common ground. If your Taurean is possessive, you'll soon feel trapped and want to break free, or decide to do things behind their back.

Sagittarius and **Gemini** is a super combination. You have masses in common and are endlessly intrigued by one another. However, you must be friends as well as lovers, otherwise you may soon get bored with each other.

Sagittarius and **Cancer** can't make each other out at all. You're mystified by your Cancerian's constant need for their home and family, and will be irritated if you think they're too parochial and unadventurous.

Sagittarius and **Leo** revel in each other's company, especially when it comes to having fun. This can be an expensive pairing because you both enjoy living it up whenever you get the chance. Shopping trips will also be costly.

Sagittarius and **Virgo** is OK up to a point. You enjoy each other's brains but you'll soon lose patience if your Virgo is very finicky and anxious. You like to let your hair down but they may always worry about the consequences.

Sagittarius and **Libra** like each other, whether as friends, family or lovers. You have enough similarities to find some common ground but enough differences to keep things interesting. It's an intriguing combination.

Sagittarius and **Scorpio** try and fail to understand each other. You like to take life as it comes and can't stand your Scorpio's tendency to plot things in advance. You'll hate it if they're suspicious or jealous of you.

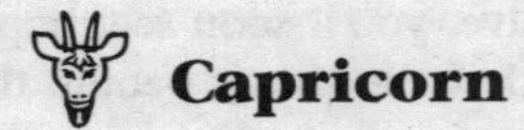

Capricorn

Capricorn and **Capricorn** feel very safe together. At last you're with someone who understands you, and who's as reliable and responsible as you. However, this may mean that your work clashes with your relationship.

Capricorn and **Aquarius** is either a big hit or a big no-no. You both need to compromise and be willing to learn from each other for it to work. Your love of convention will be sorely challenged by your radical Aquarian.

Capricorn and **Pisces** can learn a lot from each other as friends. You'll learn to be more sensitive and open-minded. However, you'll soon be turned off if your Piscean is reluctant to face up to facts and be realistic.

Capricorn and **Aries** support each other in many ways. You're both ambitious and will respect one another's goals. You'll enjoy teaching your Arien to be more responsible, and they'll teach you how to play.

Capricorn and **Taurus** feel safe with one another. You both understand the importance of tradition and share the need to do things properly. You can get surprisingly earthy and intense in the bedroom.

Capricorn and **Gemini** don't really hit it off. You're amused by your Gemini but you may secretly think they're too flighty and superficial for you. It's difficult to find much common ground sexually or emotionally.

Capricorn and **Cancer** really enjoy each other's company. You both adore having someone to take care of, and if anyone can dissuade you from working round the clock it's a home-cooking, sensuous and affectionate Cancerian.

Capricorn and **Leo** both like the best in life but you won't be as willing to pay for it as your Leo. In fact, you may be seriously worried by their extravagance and also slightly wearied by their demanding social life.

Capricorn and **Virgo** go together like bread and butter. However, there may not be much jam if you're both careful with your money. If you share a home you'll want it to be traditional, with conventional family values.

Capricorn and **Libra** have a healthy respect for each other. You love your Libran's diplomacy and tact, because you know you can take them anywhere and they'll fit in. They'll also encourage you to open up emotionally.

Capricorn and **Scorpio** is a very businesslike pairing. You excel at making money together, no matter what your relationship. Sometimes you can be put off by the intense and complex passions of your Scorpio.

Capricorn and **Sagittarius** can be strange. You like each other for your curiosity value if not much else. Even so, your Sagittarian will teach you to be more broad-minded and relaxed, if you let them.

Aquarius

Aquarius and **Aquarius** is either wonderful or too much like hard work. One if not both of you must be willing to compromise sometimes, otherwise it will be continual stalemate. You'll have formidable battles of intellect.

Aquarius and **Pisces** is tricky. You don't understand each other, and the more unworldly and unrealistic your Piscean, the more dogmatic and precise you'll become in retaliation. You can easily hurt each other.

Aquarius and **Aries** are great sparring partners and you'll love every minute of it. Your Arien isn't afraid to stand up to you and to fight their corner. They'll also teach you a thing or two about sexual relationships.

Aquarius and **Taurus** is fine all the while you agree with each other. But, at the first hint of dissent, it will be war. Your need for emotional and intellectual freedom will clash with your Taurean's need for closeness.

Aquarius and **Gemini** are firm friends. You enjoy intense intellectual discussions and your Gemini will teach you to be more free-thinking and flexible. Try not to analyse your relationship out of existence.

Aquarius and **Cancer** can be an uneasy combination. You have little in common and don't understand each other. At first you'll enjoy being taken care of by your Cancerian but you may soon feel suffocated and trapped.

Aquarius and **Leo** enjoy each other's company. You love your Leo's exuberance and marvel at their social skills. You'll also be very impressed by their ability to organize you and make your life run so smoothly.

Aquarius and **Virgo** can seem like hard work. It's easier to be friends than lovers because you have such different views of the world. You enjoy pitting your wits against each other in wide-ranging discussions.

Aquarius and **Libra** is great fun and you love sharing ideas. If you get involved in an emotional relationship, your Libran will encourage you to be more demonstrative and less analytical about your feelings.

Aquarius and **Scorpio** is a very powerful combination because you're both so sure of yourselves. In the inevitable disputes, neither of you will want to back down. You may also be turned off by your Scorpio's complicated emotions.

Aquarius and **Sagittarius** enjoy each other's company. You also share a love of learning and both need as much intellectual freedom as you can get. This can be a very enduring relationship, whether it's platonic or passionate.

Aquarius and **Capricorn** will give you lots to think about because you'll be so busy trying to work out what makes each other tick. You may never arrive at an answer! You need to find some middle ground and to compromise.

Compatibility in Love and Sex at a glance

F / M	♈	♉	♊	♋	♌	♍	♎	♏	♐	♑	♒	♓
♈	8	5	9	7	9	4	7	8	9	7	7	3
♉	6	8	4	10	7	8	8	7	3	8	2	8
♊	8	2	7	3	8	7	9	4	9	4	9	4
♋	5	10	4	8	6	5	6	8	2	9	2	8
♌	9	8	9	7	7	4	9	6	8	7	9	6
♍	4	8	6	4	4	7	6	7	7	9	4	4
♎	7	8	10	7	8	5	9	6	9	6	10	6
♏	7	9	4	7	6	6	7	10	5	6	5	7
♐	9	4	10	4	9	7	8	4	9	6	9	5
♑	7	8	4	9	6	8	6	4	4	8	4	5
♒	8	6	9	4	9	4	9	6	8	7	8	2
♓	7	6	7	9	6	7	6	9	7	5	4	9

1 = the pits
10 = the peaks

Key

♈ – Aries
♉ – Taurus
♊ – Gemini
♋ – Cancer
♌ – Leo
♍ – Virgo
♎ – Libra
♏ – Scorpio
♐ – Sagittarius
♑ – Capricorn
♒ – Aquarius
♓ – Pisces

Compatibility in Friendship at a glance

M \ F	♈	♉	♊	♋	♌	♍	♎	♏	♐	♑	♒	♓
♈	8	5	10	5	9	3	7	8	9	6	8	5
♉	6	9	6	10	7	8	7	6	4	9	3	9
♊	9	3	9	4	9	8	10	5	10	5	10	6
♋	6	9	4	9	5	4	6	9	4	10	3	9
♌	10	7	9	6	9	4	8	6	9	6	9	7
♍	5	9	8	4	4	8	5	8	8	10	5	6
♎	8	9	10	8	8	6	9	5	9	6	10	7
♏	7	8	5	8	7	7	6	9	4	5	6	8
♐	9	5	10	4	10	8	8	4	10	7	9	6
♑	6	9	5	10	6	9	5	5	4	9	5	6
♒	9	6	10	5	9	5	9	7	9	5	9	3
♓	6	7	6	10	6	8	7	9	8	6	4	10

1 = the pits
10 = the peaks

Key

♈ - Aries
♉ - Taurus
♊ - Gemini
♋ - Cancer
♌ - Leo
♍ - Virgo
♎ - Libra
♏ - Scorpio
♐ - Sagittarius
♑ - Capricorn
♒ - Aquarius
♓ - Pisces

YOUR ASTROLOGICAL HOLIDAY GUIDE

Have you ever wondered which holiday destination is right for your Sun sign, and what sort of activities you'll most enjoy when you get there? Well, your questions have been answered because this guide will give you some great ideas about how to have the holiday of a lifetime.

Pisces

You're so sensitive to atmospheres that you need to choose your holiday destination very carefully. Try to avoid political trouble spots or places that are heaving with fellow holiday-makers because your delicate nerves will soon become jangled and you'll start longing to go home again. You adore being near water, whether it's a lake or an ocean, and find it very relaxing just to listen to the sound of the waves while gazing into space. The clear blue waters of a tropical island would be paradise for you, because you love swimming. You aren't comfortable if you have to rough it, so are happiest staying somewhere that offers plenty of luxury. However, you'll be very disturbed if there's a marked contrast between your level of comfort and that of the local people. Your ideal holiday includes plenty of sightseeing, because you love soaking up the atmosphere and getting a strong sense of the spirit of the place.

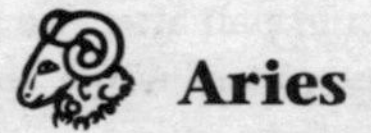

Aries

In an ideal world, you would never visit the same holiday destination twice because you hate that sense of 'been there, done that'. Besides, there's a whole world out there waiting to be explored, so why waste your valuable holiday time going back to the same old resort year after year? If you're a typical Arien, excitement, heat and plenty of action are the ingredients for a perfect holiday. If a little courage is required, then so much the better. You'll enjoy regaling your friends and family with eye-popping tales of your bravery as you mastered white-water rafting, braved huge rollers on your surfboard, went on safari, trekked through a jungle or endured the baking heat of a desert. If you have to choose something that you consider to be more tame, you'll enjoy a fly-drive or activity holiday. At a pinch, you might be persuaded to lie on a beach but you won't want to do it for long because you'll soon get bored.

Taurus

As the great hedonist of the zodiac, your idea of a blissful holiday is one in which you do as little as possible while other people attend to your every whim. If money is no object you'll be in seventh heaven staying in a luxury hotel that serves delectable drinks, sumptuous food and has the finest cotton sheets. Some signs are completely incapable of sitting around doing nothing but you could turn it into an art form, given half a chance. If you have to lower your holiday sights through a lack of cash, you'd enjoy staying in a self-catering cottage in beautiful surroundings. The cottage must have all mod cons, of course, because the charm of pumping your own water from a tumbledown well would pall after the first ten minutes. You feel revived and rejuvenated when you're surrounded by nature and beauty, so you might enjoy a holiday tour of famous gardens, a visit to a country renowned for its autumn colours or a trip to an unspoilt island paradise.

Gemini

Variety is the spice of life for you, so you won't want to visit the same destination year after year. Instead, you like the thought of trying somewhere completely different each time, because half the fun is reading about it before you go and then trying to cram a selection of indispensable travel guides and phrase books into your already bulging suitcase. You need to keep on the move, too, so are happiest if the local transport is excellent or you can hire a car to get around. You're thrilled by bustling cities, especially if you can sit in a café and watch the world go by, then shop to your heart's content. Destinations that are steeped in history or culture also appeal to you. Another option is to take an activity holiday in which you'll learn something new; it could be anything from watercolour painting to belly-dancing.

Cancer

Familiarity breeds content for you, so you can feel uneasy when visiting somewhere for the first time. What if you don't like it? You're the sort of person who is welcomed with open arms by hoteliers because if you like the place you'll return year after year, and you'll take your nearest and dearest with you. It's a rare Cancerian who doesn't enjoy eating, so you'll want to choose a destination in which the food is to your liking, and you'll hope that there's lots of it. You can't cope with anything too exotic or strange, and you need to take care of your sensitive tummy, which rules out some of the more far-flung corners of the world. You also can't tolerate extreme heat or humidity. You love being near water and would enjoy a relaxing beach holiday or staying at a hotel on a large lake. Another option is a self-catering holiday in which you can create a home from home.

Leo

The one thing you crave above all else is sunshine, so it's very high up on your list of holiday priorities. You really come into your own when you're in a hot climate, although even you will wilt if the temperature rises too high. If you could have your heart's desire, you'd stay in a luxurious and exclusive resort on a tropical island, where you could do lots of celebrity-spotting while sipping cocktails on a palm-fringed beach. Too expensive? Then you would love going on safari and seeing your namesake lions prowling around, provided you didn't have to hammer in your own tent pegs every night. You do have your standards! Something else that would appeal is driving through a warm and friendly country in a chic or classic car, staying at delightful hotels along the way and buying lots of lovely clothes to wear when you get home.

Virgo

Although you may sound enthusiastic when your friends tell you about their trips to exotic locations, or describe meals containing the sort of wriggly items that you would squash to death if you found them in your garden, in reality you avoid them like the plague. Actually, you would probably rather have the plague than visit anywhere with dodgy hygiene, unsafe drinking water, poisonous creepy-crawlies, stomach-churning food or primitive plumbing. You're not the most adventurous traveller in the world and you don't care! Ideal holiday destinations for you include ski resorts where you can get exercise, hot chocolate and fresh air, or luxurious health farms that serve more than just a single lettuce leaf once a day. You would also adore a specialist holiday which caters for one of your interests and keeps your very clever brain fully occupied.

Libra

You can take any amount of luxury, relaxation and lotus-eating, especially when you're on holiday. You're too intelligent to be content spending a fortnight lying on a beach, but you might fancy visiting somewhere that offers the twin attractions of sparkling blue seas and plenty of culture. Decent food will also be high on your list of holiday essentials, because there's nothing you like better than working your way through a menu full of delicious temptations. You may even choose your destination or hotel purely on the strength of its cuisine or wine, and you'll do your best to sample as much of it as possible. If you're a typical Libran you have very sophisticated tastes and would enjoy visiting one of the great cities of the world, especially if you can combine sightseeing with an enjoyable tour of the best shops you can find.

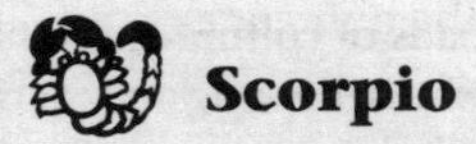

Scorpio

You take such an intense approach to life that regular breaks are essential for you, because they help you to get things back in perspective. What's more, you're prepared to spend quite a lot of money on a holiday if necessary. If you can only take a short break, you adore the thought of staying in a fabulous country hotel, complete with spa, swimming pool, gardens and Michelin-starred dining room. So what if the bill makes your eyes water? You'll have had more than your money's worth in terms of enjoyment. You soon get bored if nothing is going on, so an activity holiday is perfect for you, especially if it offers plenty of excitement. You could learn to scuba-dive, brush up your skiing, go potholing or practise body-surfing. If you fancy something less daredevil, you might consider a wine-tasting holiday, a murder-mystery weekend or an Antarctic cruise.

Sagittarius

If you're a dyed-in-the-wool Sagittarian, you've probably already chosen the destinations of your next ten holidays. Travel is in your blood and you love exploring the world. You're unlikely to want to revisit the same place twice, although you might develop an abiding passion for a particular country and enjoy visiting different parts of it over the years. In the end, you'll be quite an expert on the subject. Your ideal holiday offers a combination of delicious food and drink, breathtaking scenery, comfortable sleeping arrangements, plenty of history, loads of culture and lots to look at. Grilling on a beach for two weeks, looking only at the sand, is your idea of hell. You'd much rather jump on a local bus and see where it takes you, laze the afternoon away in a restaurant or put your guidebook through its paces. You enjoy both heat and cold, which means you can be happy almost anywhere in the world.

Capricorn

You aren't entirely convinced by the need for holidays because they can seem like such an extravagance to you. Deep down, you'd probably rather stay at home and feel good about the money you've saved. If you are persuaded to go away, you won't want to throw your cash around willy-nilly and will choose somewhere that doesn't cost the earth. Nevertheless, you aren't keen on places that are too cheap and cheerful, and you're quite choosy about the company you keep. You might enjoy a skiing holiday, rock climbing or simply relaxing high in the mountains somewhere. You're very practical, so would also appreciate a holiday in which you learn a new skill or craft. You have a strong conservative streak, so will avoid anywhere that's too exotic, strange or dangerous. Instead, you'll choose places that feel familiar, and preferably where there's no language barrier.

Aquarius

The last thing you want to do on holiday is be surrounded by crowds and feel that you're part of a gigantic marketing machine. Instead, you're drawn to places that are off the beaten track, unfashionable (so you don't have to rub shoulders with every Tom, Dick and Harry) or are yet to be discovered by most people. You have no interest in simple beach holidays, unless you can alternate sunbathing with plenty of sightseeing. Destinations steeped in history and culture are ideal for you, because you love tuning in to the atmosphere and learning more about the country you're visiting. It's also essential that the place offers peace and quiet, so you can read all those books you've brought with you. For you, part of the pleasure of going on holiday is meeting the locals, so it's important that you visit somewhere friendly and welcoming.

BORN ON THE CUSP?

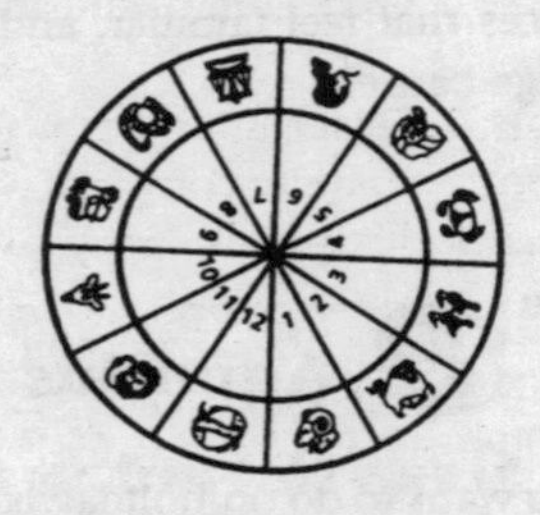

Were you born on the cusp of Pisces – at the beginning or end of the sign? If so, you may have spent years wondering which sign you belong to. Are you a Piscean, an Aquarian or an Arien? Different horoscope books and columns can give different dates for when the Sun moves into each sign, leaving you utterly confused. Yet none of these dates is wrong, as you'll discover in a minute. Checking your birth date, and time if you know it, in the list given in this chapter will allow you to solve the mystery at long last!

Many people believe that the Sun moves like clockwork from one sign to another on a specific day each year. But this isn't always true. For instance, let's look at the dates for the sign of Pisces. On the cover of this book I give them as 19 February to 20 March. Very often, the Sun will obediently change signs on these days but sometimes it won't. It can move from Aquarius into Pisces on 18 or 19 February and it can move into Aries on 20 or 21 March.

So how can you find out which sign you belong to if you were born on the cusp of Pisces? The only information you need is the place, year, day and the time of your birth if you know it. It helps to have the time of birth because if the Sun did move signs on your birthday, you can see whether it moved before or after you were born. If you don't have an exact time, even knowing whether it was morning or afternoon can be a help. For instance, if you were born in the morning and the Sun didn't move signs on your birthday until the afternoon, that will be enough information to tell you which sign is yours.

You need to know the place in case you were born outside the United Kingdom and have to convert its local time zone to British time. This information is easily available in many diaries and reference books.

Four Simple Steps to Find your Sun Sign

1. Write down the year, day, time and place of your birth, in that order.
2. If you were born outside the United Kingdom, you must convert your birth date and time to British time by adding or subtracting the relevant number of hours. This may take your birthday into the following day or back to the previous day. If so, write down this new date and time because that will be the one you use in the following calculations. If summer time was operating you must deduct the relevant number of hours to convert your birth time to Greenwich Mean Time (GMT).
3. If you were born in Britain, look up your year of birth in the list of British Summer Time (BST) changes to see if BST was operating when you were born. If it was, subtract the appropriate number of hours from your birth time to convert it to GMT. This may give you a different time and/or date of birth.
4. Look up your year of birth in the Annual Sun Sign Changes list. If you were born within these dates and times, you are a Piscean. If you were born outside them, you are either an Aquarian if you were born in February, or an Arien if you were born in March.

Two Examples

Here are a couple of examples so you can see how the process works. Let's say we're looking for the Sun sign of Jean, who was born in the UK on 19 February 1968 at 00:40. Start by checking the list of British Summer Time (BST) dates to see if BST was operating at the time of her birth. It was, so you have to subtract one hour from her birth time to convert it to GMT. This gives her a birth time of 23:40 on the previous day – therefore, her GMT birthday is 18 February and her GMT birth time is 23:40. Write this down, so you don't forget it. Now turn to the Annual Sun Sign Changes list and look for 1968, her year of birth. In that year, the Sun moved into Pisces on 19 February at 14:10, and Jean's GMT birth was the previous evening, so she is an Aquarian. However, if she had been born on 19 February 1970 (note the change of year) at 03:30 (which gives her a GMT birth time of 02:30), the Sun would have been in Pisces so she would be a Piscean.

But what would her sign be if she were born on 20 March 1981 at 18:45? First, check the dates in the BST list for 1981 to see if it was operating at the time of her birth. It wasn't, so her birth time and day remain the same. Now look up the Sun sign dates for 1981. Look at the March date. The Sun was in Pisces until 20 March at 17:03. So Jean was born just after the Sun had moved into Aries, making her an Arien.

Dates for British Summer Time

If your birthday falls within these dates and times, you were born during BST and will have to convert your birth time back to GMT. To do this, subtract one hour from your birth time. If you were born during a period that is marked *, you must subtract two hours from your birth time to convert it to GMT. All times are given in BST, using the 24-hour clock.

1920 28 Mar, 02:00–25 Oct, 01:59 inc
1921 3 Apr, 02:00–3 Oct, 01:59 inc
1922 26 Mar, 02:00–8 Oct, 01:59 inc
1923 22 Apr, 02:00–16 Sep, 01:59 inc
1924 13 Apr, 02:00–21 Sep, 01:59 inc
1925 19 Apr, 02:00–4 Oct, 01:59 inc
1926 18 Apr, 02:00–3 Oct, 01:59 inc
1927 10 Apr, 02:00–2 Oct, 01:59 inc
1928 22 Apr, 02:00–7 Oct, 01:59 inc
1929 21 Apr, 02:00–6 Oct, 01:59 inc
1930 13 Apr, 02:00–5 Oct, 01:59 inc
1931 19 Apr, 02:00–4 Oct, 01:59 inc
1932 17 Apr, 02:00–2 Oct, 01:59 inc
1933 9 Apr, 02:00–8 Oct, 01:59 inc
1934 22 Apr, 02:00–7 Oct, 01:59 inc
1935 14 Apr, 02:00–6 Oct, 01:59 inc
1936 19 Apr, 02:00–4 Oct, 01:59 inc
1937 18 Apr, 02:00–3 Oct, 01:59 inc
1938 10 Apr, 02:00–2 Oct, 01:59 inc
1939 16 Apr, 02:00–19 Nov, 01:59 inc
1940 25 Feb, 02:00–31 Dec, 23:59 inc
1941 1 Jan, 00:00–4 May, 01:59 inc
1941 4 May, 02:00–10 Aug, 01:59 inc*
1941 10 Aug, 02:00–31 Dec, 23:59 inc
1942 1 Jan, 00:00–5 Apr, 01:59 inc
1942 5 Apr, 02:00–9 Aug, 01:59 inc*
1942 9 Aug, 02:00–31 Dec, 23:59 inc
1943 1 Jan, 00:00–4 Apr, 01:59 inc
1943 4 Apr, 02:00–15 Aug, 01:59 inc*
1943 15 Aug, 02:00–31 Dec, 23:59 inc
1944 1 Jan, 00:00–2 Apr, 01:59 inc
1944 2 Apr, 02:00–17 Sep, 01:59 inc*
1944 17 Sep, 02:00–31 Dec, 23:59 inc
1945 1 Jan, 02:00–2 Apr, 01:59 inc
1945 2 Apr, 02:00–15 Jul, 01:59 inc*
1945 15 Jul, 02:00–7 Oct, 01:59 inc
1946 14 Apr, 02:00–6 Oct, 01:59 inc
1947 16 Mar, 02:00–13 Apr, 01:59 inc
1947 13 Apr, 02:00–10 Aug, 01:59 inc*
1947 10 Aug, 02:00–2 Nov, 01:59 inc
1948 14 Mar, 02:00–31 Oct, 01:59 inc
1949 3 Apr, 02:00–30 Oct, 01:59 inc
1950 16 Apr, 02:00–22 Oct, 01:59 inc
1951 15 Apr, 02:00–21 Oct, 01:59 inc
1952 20 Apr, 02:00–26 Oct, 01:59 inc
1953 19 Apr, 02:00–4 Oct, 01:59 inc
1954 11 Apr, 02:00–3 Oct, 01:59 inc
1955 17 Apr, 02:00–2 Oct, 01:59 inc
1956 22 Apr, 02:00–7 Oct, 01:59 inc
1957 14 Apr, 02:00–6 Oct, 01:59 inc
1958 20 Apr, 02:00–5 Oct, 01:59 inc
1959 19 Apr, 02:00–4 Oct, 01:59 inc
1960 10 Apr, 02:00–2 Oct, 01:59 inc
1961 26 Mar, 02:00–29 Oct, 01:59 inc
1962 25 Mar, 02:00–28 Oct, 01:59 inc
1963 31 Mar, 02:00–27 Oct, 01:59 inc
1964 22 Mar, 02:00–25 Oct, 01:59 inc
1965 21 Mar, 02:00–24 Oct, 01:59 inc
1966 20 Mar, 02:00–23 Oct, 01:59 inc
1967 19 Mar, 02:00–29 Oct, 01:59 inc
1968 18 Feb, 02:00–31 Dec, 23:59 inc
1969 1 Jan, 00:00–31 Dec, 23:59 inc
1970 1 Jan, 00:00–31 Dec, 23:59 inc
1971 1 Jan, 00:00–31 Oct, 01:59 inc
1972 19 Mar, 02:00–29 Oct, 01:59 inc
1973 18 Mar, 02:00–28 Oct, 01:59 inc
1974 17 Mar, 02:00–27 Oct, 01:59 inc
1975 16 Mar, 02:00–26 Oct, 01:59 inc
1976 21 Mar, 02:00–24 Oct, 01:59 inc
1977 20 Mar, 02:00–23 Oct, 01:59 inc
1978 19 Mar, 02:00–29 Oct, 01:59 inc
1979 18 Mar, 02:00–28 Oct, 01:59 inc
1980 16 Mar, 02:00–26 Oct, 01:59 inc
1981 29 Mar, 01:00–25 Oct, 00:59 inc
1982 28 Mar, 01:00–24 Oct, 00:59 inc
1983 27 Mar, 01:00–23 Oct, 00:59 inc
1984 25 Mar, 01:00–28 Oct, 00:59 inc
1985 31 Mar, 01:00–27 Oct, 00:59 inc
1986 30 Mar, 01:00–26 Oct, 00:59 inc
1987 29 Mar, 01:00–25 Oct, 00:59 inc
1988 27 Mar, 01:00–23 Oct, 00:59 inc
1989 26 Mar, 01:00–29 Oct, 00:59 inc
1990 25 Mar, 01:00–28 Oct, 00:59 inc
1991 31 Mar, 01:00–27 Oct, 00:59 inc
1992 29 Mar, 01:00–25 Oct, 00:59 inc
1993 28 Mar, 01:00–24 Oct, 00:59 inc
1994 27 Mar, 01:00–23 Oct, 00:59 inc
1995 26 Mar, 01:00–22 Oct, 00:59 inc

1996 31 Mar, 01:00–27 Oct, 00:59 inc
1997 30 Mar, 01:00–26 Oct, 00:59 inc
1998 29 Mar, 01:00–25 Oct, 00:59 inc
1999 28 Mar, 01:00–31 Oct, 00:59 inc
2000 26 Mar, 01:00–29 Oct, 00:59 inc
2001 25 Mar, 01:00–28 Oct, 00:59 inc
2002 31 Mar, 01:00–27 Oct, 00:59 inc
2003 30 Mar, 01:00–26 Oct, 00:59 inc
2004 28 Mar, 01:00–31 Oct, 00:59 inc

* Subtract two hours from the birth time to convert it to GMT.

Annual Sun Sign Changes

If your birthday falls within these dates and times, you are a Piscean. If you were born in February before the first date and time, you are an Aquarian. If you were born in March after the second date and time, you are an Arien. All times are given in GMT, using the 24-hour clock.

1920 19 Feb, 22:29–20 Mar, 21:59 inc
1921 19 Feb, 04:20–21 Mar, 03:50 inc
1922 19 Feb, 10:17–21 Mar, 09:46 inc
1923 19 Feb, 16:00–21 Mar, 15:28 inc
1924 19 Feb, 21:52–20 Mar, 21:20 inc
1925 19 Feb, 03:43–21 Mar, 03:12 inc
1926 19 Feb, 09:35–21 Mar, 09:01 inc
1927 19 Feb, 15:35–21 Mar, 14:59 inc
1928 19 Feb, 21:20–20 Mar, 20:44 inc
1929 19 Feb, 03:07–21 Mar, 02:34 inc
1930 19 Feb, 09:00–21 Mar, 08:29 inc
1931 19 Feb, 14:41–21 Mar, 14:06 inc
1932 19 Feb, 20:29–20 Mar, 19:53 inc
1933 19 Feb, 02:17–21 Mar, 01:43 inc
1934 19 Feb, 08:02–21 Mar, 07:27 inc
1935 19 Feb, 13:52–21 Mar, 13:17 inc
1936 19 Feb, 19:33–20 Mar, 18:57 inc
1937 19 Feb, 01:21–21 Mar, 00:44 inc
1938 19 Feb, 07:20–21 Mar, 06:42 inc
1939 19 Feb, 13:10–21 Mar, 12:28 inc
1940 19 Feb, 19:04–20 Mar, 18:23 inc
1941 19 Feb, 00:57–21 Mar, 00:20 inc
1942 19 Feb, 06:47–21 Mar, 06:10 inc
1943 19 Feb, 12:41–21 Mar, 12:02 inc
1944 19 Feb, 18:28–20 Mar, 17:48 inc
1945 19 Feb, 00:15–20 Mar, 23:37 inc
1946 19 Feb, 06:09–21 Mar, 05:32 inc
1947 19 Feb, 11:52–21 Mar, 11:12 inc
1948 19 Feb, 17:37–20 Mar, 16:56 inc
1949 18 Feb, 23:28–20 Mar, 22:48 inc
1950 19 Feb, 05:18–21 Mar, 04:35 inc
1951 19 Feb, 11:10–21 Mar, 10:25 inc
1952 19 Feb, 16:57–20 Mar, 16:13 inc
1953 18 Feb, 22:42–20 Mar, 22:00 inc
1954 19 Feb, 04:33–21 Mar, 03:53 inc
1955 19 Feb, 10:19–21 Mar, 09:35 inc
1956 19 Feb, 16:05–20 Mar, 15:20 inc
1957 18 Feb, 21:59–20 Mar, 21:16 inc
1958 19 Feb, 03:49–21 Mar, 03:05 inc
1959 19 Feb, 09:38–21 Mar, 08:54 inc
1960 19 Feb, 15:27–20 Mar, 14:42 inc
1961 18 Feb, 21:17–20 Mar, 20:32 inc
1962 19 Feb, 03:15–21 Mar, 02:29 inc
1963 19 Feb, 09:09–21 Mar, 08:19 inc
1964 19 Feb, 14:58–20 Mar, 14:09 inc
1965 18 Feb, 20:48–20 Mar, 20:04 inc
1966 19 Feb, 02:38–21 Mar, 01:53 inc
1967 19 Feb, 08:24–21 Mar, 07:36 inc
1968 19 Feb, 14:10–20 Mar, 13:22 inc
1969 18 Feb, 19:55–20 Mar, 19:08 inc
1970 19 Feb, 01:42–21 Mar, 00:56 inc
1971 19 Feb, 07:28–21 Mar, 06:38 inc
1972 19 Feb, 13:12–20 Mar, 12:21 inc
1973 18 Feb, 19:02–20 Mar, 18:12 inc
1974 19 Feb, 00:59–21 Mar, 00:06 inc
1975 19 Feb, 06:50–21 Mar, 05:56 inc

1976 19 Feb, 12:41–20 Mar, 11:49 inc
1977 18 Feb, 18:31–20 Mar, 17:42 inc
1978 19 Feb, 00:22–20 Mar, 23:33 inc
1979 19 Feb, 06:14–21 Mar, 05:22 inc
1980 19 Feb, 12:03–20 Mar, 11:10 inc
1981 18 Feb, 17:53–20 Mar, 17:03 inc
1982 18 Feb, 23:47–20 Mar, 22:56 inc
1983 19 Feb, 05:31–21 Mar, 04:39 inc
1984 19 Feb, 11:17–20 Mar, 10:24 inc
1985 18 Feb, 17:08–20 Mar, 16:14 inc
1986 18 Feb, 22:58–20 Mar, 22:03 inc
1987 19 Feb, 04:51–21 Mar, 03:52 inc
1988 19 Feb, 10:36–20 Mar, 09:39 inc
1989 18 Feb, 16:21–20 Mar, 15:28 inc
1990 18 Feb, 22:15–20 Mar, 21:19 inc
1991 19 Feb, 03:59–21 Mar, 03:02 inc
1992 19 Feb, 09:44–20 Mar, 08:48 inc
1993 18 Feb, 15:36–20 Mar, 14:41 inc
1994 18 Feb, 21:23–20 Mar, 20:28 inc
1995 19 Feb, 03:12–21 Mar, 02:14 inc
1996 19 Feb, 09:02–20 Mar, 08:03 inc
1997 18 Feb, 14:53–20 Mar, 13:55 inc
1998 18 Feb, 20:56–20 Mar, 19:55 inc
1999 19 Feb, 02:48–21 Mar, 01:46 inc
2000 19 Feb, 08:34–20 Mar, 07:35 inc
2001 18 Feb, 14:28–20 Mar, 13:31 inc
2002 18 Feb, 20:14–20 Mar, 19:16 inc
2003 19 Feb, 02:01–21 Mar, 01:01 inc
2004 19 Feb, 07:51–20 Mar, 06:49 inc

Laura